SUBSTANCE
ABUSE
PROGRAM
ACCREDITATION
GUIDE

SUBSTANCE
ABUSE
PROGRAM
ACCREDITATION
GUIDE

edited by

ELIZABETH D. BROWN
TIMOTHY J. O'FARRELL
STEPHEN A. MAISTO
KAREN BOIES-HICKMAN
RICHARD SUCHINSKY

SAGE Publications
International Educational and Professional Publisher
Thousand Oaks   London   New Delhi

Copyright © 1997 by Sage Publications, Inc.

For information:

SAGE Publications, Inc.
2455 Teller Road
Thousand Oaks, California 91320
E-mail: order@sagepub.com

SAGE Publications Ltd.
6 Bonhill Street
London EC2A 4PU
United Kingdom

SAGE Publications India Pvt. Ltd.
M-32 Market
Greater Kailash I
New Delhi 110 048 India

Printed in the United States of America

Library of Congress Cataloging-in-Publication Data

Main entry under title:

Substance abuse program accreditation guide / editors, Elizabeth D.
  Brown . . . [et al.].
      p.   cm.
  Includes bibliographical references and index.
  ISBN 0-7619-0564-2 (pbk.: alk. paper)
    1. Substance abuse—Treatment—Accreditation—United States.
  I. Brown, Elizabeth D.
  RC564.73.S926   1997
  362.29′18′0973—dc21   96-51238

97 98 99 00 01 02 03 10 9 8 7 6 5 4 3 2 1

Acquiring Editor:	Jim Nageotte
Editorial Assistant:	Kathleen Derby
Production Editor:	Astrid Virding
Production Assistant:	Karen Wiley
Typesetter/Designer:	Janelle LeMaster
Cover Designer:	Candice Harman
Print Buyer:	Anna Chin

Contents

PART II: ORGANIZATIONAL FUNCTIONS

PART III: PULLING IT TOGETHER

.

Acknowledgments

We express our sincere thanks to all who assisted in the preparation of this book. Patricia Hutchins, the secretary for the Psychology Service at the Brockton/West Roxbury Veterans Affairs (VA) Medical Center, cheerfully and competently pulled material together, arranged meetings and telephone calls, and produced useful graphic materials. Robert Dewey, the program analyst for the Special Projects in Substance Abuse in the Mental Health and Strategic Health Planning arm of the Department of Veterans Affairs, was instrumental in forming an earlier group that worked on many of the topics covered in this book. From the early group, contributions by Sandra Chipman, ACSW, formerly of the Fayetteville, North Carolina, VA Medical Center, and by Mary Lou Hale, MD, Chief of the Psychiatry Service at Wilmington, Delaware, had an influence on the development of this book. Comments and reviews on our early drafts by Judith Lowe, PhD, Manager of the Outpatient Substance Abuse Treatment Program at the Brockton/West Roxbury VA Medical Center, and by Lynne Cannavo, RN, Quality Assurance Coordinator at the Brockton/West Roxbury VA Medical Center, were very helpful. We also want to acknowledge the helpful administrative support that we received from Patricia Danner, program assistant to the Deputy Chief of Staff for Mental Health at the Brockton/West Roxbury VA Medical Center; from Barbara Van Wagner, program assistant for the Counseling for Alcoholic Marriages Program at the Brockton/West Roxbury VA Medical Center; and from Lisa Rolak of the Medical Administration Service at Brockton/West Roxbury VA Medical Center. Finally, the patience of Judy Lattimore and Robert Gaines in assisting with computer applications in VA headquarters is worthy of note and thanks.

Introduction

Substance abuse treatment programs (SATPs) need to gain and maintain accreditation by the Joint Commission on Accreditation of Healthcare Organizations (hereafter referred to as Joint Commission) to receive treatment payment from government and from private third-party payers. However, program personnel at times experience uncertainty about how to meet accreditation criteria. This uncertainty may lead to one of two errors. First, staff may err on the conservative side by diverting too much staff time to Joint Commission preparations. This diversion can add considerably to a program's cost and can remove some clinician time from care activities. Second, staff may underestimate what the program needs to get accreditation. In this instance, staff may have to face the anxiety associated with a second focused survey.

In 1995 the Joint Commission published accreditation standards in a significantly changed format. Besides a new format for evaluating patient care, there were completely revised sets of standards that covered organizational aspects of programs of care. Moreover, the scoring guidelines were no longer specific to SATPs in that they addressed a range of treatment programs. In sum, the wide scope of the material, encompassing both patient care and organizational elements, was daunting.

In writing the present Accreditation Guide for meeting the new standards, we consider various kinds of programs. We cover the needs of complex SATPs that may exist in some broader medical setting or parent organization. In such settings, program leaders may have fewer responsibilities for meeting standards such as those delineated under the "Organizational Functions" section of the Joint Commission's *1995 Accredi-*

tation Manual for Mental Health, Chemical Dependency, and Mental Retardation/Developmental Disabilities Services (MHM) (Joint Commission, 1995).[1] For instance, large-scale medical operations are more likely to have experts and resources external to the program for managing computerized programs of information, for risk management, and for surveillance. We have also considered freestanding substance abuse sites in which program leadership may have to be conversant on more topics than their peers who have the assistance of the administrative side of a large medical center. Finally, in addressing standards related to denial of reimbursement for care because of determinations made by insurance companies or managed-care firms, we include public agencies in which care is sometimes more a matter of eligibility than of payment.

The Joint Commission's main purpose is to give its stamp of approval to programs that are providing respectful, ethical, and acceptable assessment, care, and education to their patients and patients' families. In keeping with the importance of quality of patient care, the standards relevant to components of patient care appear as the first five sets of standards. Acceptable care consists of a continuum of services that can provide a range of services extending from pretreatment to treatment to follow-up. Therefore, in evaluating the adequacy of a program's continuum of care, surveyors expect evidence that it affords access to an integrated system of treatment environments, interventions, and care levels. Further, surveyors expect patients' needs to be considered in deciding where in the system treatment should take place. To use a format compatible with that used by the Joint Commission, Part I of this book covers the same elements of patient care. Thus these first five chapters address in turn patient rights and responsibilities, continuum of care, assessment, patient care, and education. Throughout Part I, we provide examples and recommendations for the sundry activities of assessment, treatment planning, treatment, and education of patients and their families. We also describe how the emphasis on these activities may differ as a function of where the patient is in the continuum of care. Finally, we include information about the types of background materials that you may use to show surveyors that accreditation criteria have been carefully considered and met.

Until recently, surveyors' assessments of quality of care have focused most on the body of work produced by individual care providers.

Some systems-level evaluation did occur in areas such as program guidance materials, staff credentialing, and staff education. However, with the new standards, the Joint Commission has introduced a significant change in evaluating care in that major attention is now allocated to the performance of the entire system and its processes. The extension of the survey to include systemic or organizational factors does not eliminate Joint Commission concern about individual performance; indeed, an expectation remains that clinically competent individuals are part of the organization. Rather, the change assumes that most difficulties encountered in patient care delivery and most opportunities for improving care are beyond the responsibility of the individual and require intervention at a systems level.

When evaluating organizational functions, accreditation visitors examine the structures and processes that you use in six areas of performance: (a) the structures and processes that you apply in improving your system and care provision; (b) leadership—specifically, whether leaders provide the structure and program administrative activities that are critical to developing, delivering, and evaluating good health care; (c) whether you have a safe and supportive environment for patients and staff; (d) the management of human resources—specifically, whether you have an atmosphere conducive to staff self-development for the purpose of improving care; (e) management of information—that is, the processes by which and the quality with which health care providers communicate; and (f) surveillance, prevention, and control of infection.

Before moving to a discussion of how to meet the standards, we offer two caveats. First, in writing this book, we have taken a comprehensive view of the range of treatment and quality assurance requirements associated with SATPs. However, it is not meant to be prescriptive for staff working in SATPs. Second, although we believe that recommendations given in this book should be acceptable to any Joint Commission surveyor, the individual variation that site visitors bring to accreditation decisions always introduces some element of uncertainty. Therefore, you should gain personal familiarity with the criteria in the *MHM* for a thorough knowledge of Joint Commission criteria to maximize the likelihood of a favorable accreditation visit. We strongly recommend that you secure a copy of both the criteria and the scoring guidelines for the *MHM* from the Joint Commission.

Note

1. The *MHM* is published in two volumes. The first addresses the accreditation process more philosophically and theoretically; the second, which contains the scoring guidelines, is more of a "hands-on" approach. Both, however, contain the standards listed and discussed in this book; they merely cover this material from different perspectives. Therefore, references to the *MHM* in this book do not specify volume unless the material cited is a quote found only in one volume or the other.

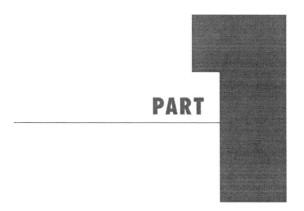

PART

Patient-Focused Functions

CHAPTER 1

Patient Rights and Responsibilities and Organizational Ethics

Elizabeth D. Brown
Stephen A. Maisto
Karen Boies-Hickman

This chapter includes two major sections: standards concerning patient rights and responsibilities and standards on organizational ethics. This set of six standards concerning patient rights and responsibilities covers a considerable amount of information. A synopsis is presented in Table 1.1.

Table 1.1   Key Points in Addressing Patient Rights and Responsibilities

Respect Patients' Right to Care (RI.1)

    Rules of patient eligibility for care
    Procedures to refer patients for services not offered by your programs
       and data to reflect their use

Address Patients' Involvement in Their Care (RI.1)

    Obtaining informed consent
    The use of family or surrogate decision makers
    Decisions to participate in investigational studies or clinical trials
    Formulation of advanced directives
    Patient involvement in treatment planning
    Patient information about the course of treatment

Provide for the Consideration of Patients' Other Needs (RI.1)

    Confidentiality of information
    Privacy and security
    Communication needs
    Resolution of complaints

Additional Standards

    Conduct of research, experimentation, and clinical trials (RI.2)
    Patient work programs (RI.3)
    Determination of need for protective services (RI.4)
    Determination of need for guardianship and access of personal advocate (RI.5)
    Use of special treatment procedures (RI.6)

Patient Rights and Responsibilities (RI.1)

Mechanisms to Respect the Patient's Rights to Care

In the ever-changing terrain of health care coverage, it is especially important that rules concerning eligibility for treatment be clearly expressed and accessible to your staff. Such rules should be set forth in a policy and procedure memorandum that covers both patient characteristics and more systemic factors such as local program rules and health insurance coverage. For example, health insurance coverage may play at least as large a role as the patient's current condition in determining eligibility for inpatient substance abuse treatment. Stipulations concerning both sets of factors should be listed. A program may also determine a person's access to its services according to the recency of his or her previous exposure to them. In the case of substance abuse treatment, common examples are (a) access to detoxification services decided by the date of the last detoxification in the same setting and (b) access to full rehabilitation services decided by date of last receipt of these services.

An important concern for substance abuse treatment programs (SATPs) is treatment of one of their own staff members. Often SATP clinical staff consider themselves recovering alcohol or other drug abusers, and it is not uncommon for such staff members to "relapse" during the time they are employed. If a staff person seeks treatment in the SATP where he or she works—say, through the organization's Employee Assistance Plan (EAP)—difficult questions of advisability of that course of treatment will probably arise, either for the staff person who needs treatment or for his or her colleagues. On the other hand, treatment of a maintenance worker in an SATP's parent organization may pose fewer difficulties. In any case, it is essential that your program have policies and procedures governing these and related eventualities.

The counterpart to a clear articulation of rules of eligibility and access to a program's services is the clear articulation of a set of procedures for treatment referral of patients who do not meet criteria of eligibility for those services. Furthermore, your program should collect data showing that your staff use well-established patient screening and transfer mechanisms.

Mechanisms That Address Patients' Involvement in Their Care

You most likely will find that your treatment setting has mechanisms addressing patients' involvement in their care. For instance, there should be policy and procedure memoranda on the topics of informed consent, the use of family and/or surrogate decision makers to facilitate care decisions, decisions to participate in investigational studies and/or clinical trials, and the formulation of advance directives.

Examination of medical records should show that your patients are in fact involved in their care. Every record should show patient involvement in treatment planning, information given to the patient about the course of treatment and his or her own role in it, and patient agreement with what was proposed. Places in which you can show compliance with these requirements include progress notes; written consent for, say, Antabuse; patient contracts; and patients' signing off on their treatment plans. We suggest that you educate your staff to write relevant and sufficiently detailed progress notes about a patient's refusal of treatment and/or the resolution of conflict in decision making about treatment. We provide an example of such a note in Chapter 4.

Mechanisms to Make Decisions About the Dying Patient

Your staff must address the topic of advance directives with patients. In some cases, treatment settings have in place a mechanism by which this topic is addressed adequately during the admissions process. However, in other settings, staff may need either to develop their own mechanism or to supplement what already exists. The Joint Commission on Accreditation of Healthcare Organizations (Joint Commission) expects that each patient has written information about his or her right to formulate an advance-directive document, has access to assistance in formulating the document, has physician involvement in the decision-making process, and has access to whatever written policies and procedures exist on the topic. Your procedures for assessments should specify that the subject of advance directives be discussed during the evaluation process. If no advance directive exists, designated staff members should educate patients about the process of developing one. If staff determine that a directive does exist, they should review it with the patient to ensure that it is congruent with his or her current wishes. Staff should reflect this education or review either on assessment forms or in progress notes.

Mechanisms That Provide for Consideration of Patients' Other Needs

Four sets of consideration are covered by this standard, and each is up to your program to resolve. You need mechanisms to provide confidentiality of information, privacy and security, communication needs, and resolution of complaints. You can give staff a structure for evaluating these concerns and correcting problems in your written program guidelines, policy and procedure memoranda, and other mechanisms. You then can use these materials as part of the formal orientation to new staff to the program, and you can bring them to patients' attention through patient handbooks or, if relevant, community meetings. This last element can be valuable in that you can use community meetings as an avenue for better communication between staff and patients and as a vehicle for conflict resolution when a disagreement extends beyond the dissatisfaction of a few. In addition, you should be able to show that team meetings are on a regular schedule and that they are used to improve communication and to provide another forum for complaint resolution.

At times, you may discover unchangeable environmental factors that have a negative influence on patients' rights to privacy or confidentiality. When such factors exist, we encourage you to use ingenuity in resolving the problems. For example, a building housing an SATP was gutted and then rehabilitated. When the program moved back to its original setting, staff soon learned that the walls had been constructed with no attention to sound barriers. Patients' therapy sessions could be heard in the halls and adjoining offices. Staff resolved the problem by having carpeting laid, by hanging tapestries on walls, and by installing white-noise machines.

Your treatment facility may have a policy on patient confidentiality that you can adopt. Even so, you may find it necessary to prepare your own document because there are more stringent requirements for confidentiality for substance abuse patients. Moreover, because the problem of AIDS and HIV looms large for substance-abusing patients, you must address additional confidentiality concerns. The policy should be directive not only concerning the methods by which confidentiality should be preserved but also concerning the need for consent forms and careful documentation in the patient medical record. In particular, Joint Commission surveyors are watchful for how confidentiality is safeguarded during both the discharge planning process and the actual discharge.

Bulletin boards providing information about scheduled team and community meetings can be prominently displayed so that patients may know when to make conflicts and concerns known. You may also publish the schedule for meetings in a patient's handbook. If significant patient concerns emerge in meetings, assign a team member to write a progress note for the relevant patient's chart documenting the nature of the concern and action ensuing from the discussion.

Additional Standards

Research, Experimentation, and Clinical Trials (RI.2)

The 1995 Joint Commission standards on patient rights cover several topics that were not major considerations in the previous editions of SATP-specific standards. The first of these is the conduct of research, experimentation, and clinical trials, which typically is governed by an organization's local Investigational Review Board (IRB). Such a board may function at the level of your program or, if pertinent, at the level of the organization of which your program is a part. Policies should be written regarding the IRB's duties and responsibilities in the organization for surveyors to review. In addition, surveyors may ask to see minutes of IRB meetings. At the program level, the clinical record may be a source of data on a patient's decision to participate in a clinical investigation and, if such participation occurred, its process as relevant to the patient's care.

Appendix A of this book provides an example of an informed-consent form that has passed rigorous IRB review criteria. The form was developed for use in a clinical trial of the effectiveness of different types of brief interventions for alcohol problems that is being conducted in a major medical center and in several community primary care clinics. It is important to note how the consent form complies with RI.2.2 by addressing all of the stipulations in Standards RI.2.1.1 through RI.2.1.5.

Patient Work Programs (RI.3) and
Need for Protective Services (RI.4)

Another topic concerns patients' working for your program or for your program's parent organization. In this case, it is imperative that your staff members continue to see clinical service provision as their primary role with patients. This prioritization should be reflected in your program's policy and procedures manual, which also should detail when patient work for the program may occur. If patient work does occur, it should be presented with clear justification in the clinical record's progress notes and treatment plan. The Joint Commission also includes a standard on assisting the patient, family, and the court in determination of need for protective services. Policies must be available on staff involvement in assessing the need for such services and in education of the patient and his or her family. Evidence of such education should be available in the clinical record.

Guardianship (RI.5) and Use of
Special Treatment Procedures (RI.6)

A standard also has been included on determining the need for guardianship and on access to a personal advocate. Policies and procedures should be available on conducting an independent review to determine the need for guardianship, and the review process and outcome should be recorded in the progress notes. Similarly, policy needs to be written on accessing a personal advocate. Staff need to be trained in accessing personal advocates and in the advocate's roles and responsibilities. Besides the policy and procedures manual, evidence regarding the standard may be obtained in documentation of staff training, the clinical record, and copies of contractual agreements with personal advocacy organizations.

The final additional standard concerns provision of special treatment procedures. In substance abuse treatment, common examples of such "special treatments" might be use of anticraving or anxiolytic medications. Application of such procedures again needs to be congruent with your policy and needs justification in the clinical record.

Table 1.2 summarizes the key points covered in the patient rights and responsibilities section of this chapter, along with evidence that you may use to demonstrate compliance with the relevant standards. It is important to add that for the topics listed in Table 1.2 and for virtually all other topics of evaluation that will be identified in this book, surveyors may use staff interviews as evidence to judge compliance with standards. Also, as relevant, surveyors may choose to use interviews with patients and their significant others as data sources. Because interviews with these three sets of people could be applied to many evaluation topics, they will not be listed repeatedly. However, it should be kept in mind that they can be extremely helpful and frequently used sources of data for surveyors.

Organizational Ethics (RI.7)

The Joint Commission assesses the ethics of the organization in practices concerning marketing, admissions, transfers, discharges, and billing, and in the organization's relationship to other health providers, educational institutions, and payers. For the most part, these standards apply to the parts of your treatment setting in which billing, interactions with insurers, and relationships with affiliated universities are handled. If policies relevant to these factors are set by a parent organization, you should have some obligations related to this set of standards. For exam-

Table 1.2 Standards for Patient Rights and Evidence of Compliance

Standards	Evidence of Compliance
Rules on eligibility for care Referral procedures Use of referral procedures Patients' involvement in their care Providing for patients' other needs (e.g., confidentiality of information, privacy and security, communication needs, resolution of conflicts and complaints) Conduct of research Patient work Need for protective services Need for guardianship Use of special treatment Outreach and public relations Maintenance of relationships with professional staff in other treatment programs Maintenance of relationship with the community Examination of your continuum of care	Policy and procedures manual CQM data Clinical records (e.g., signed informed consents, patient contracts, patients' signing of treatment plans, progress notes) Written program guidelines Patient handbooks Minutes of institutional review board (IRB) meetings Minutes of clinical team meetings Documentation of staff training; contractual agreements

ple, any outreach or public relations programs that your staff initiate should be introduced with an accurate description of individuals who are eligible for and who might benefit from care. Your staff must maintain relationships with colleagues in acute psychiatry settings so that appropriate care can be arranged for patients who are determined to be a risk to themselves or others. Relationships must be maintained with SATPs at other sites so that patients can be transferred when another site is more suited to their care. Ties must be maintained with community groups, self-help groups, and aftercare supports (such as halfway houses). Finally, we suggest that you examine your continuum of care to ensure that patients can move through it smoothly. If impediments to movement are found, you can take steps to correct the problem. Joint Commission surveyors may look in a number of places to determine compliance with the standards. You can produce minutes of meetings showing attention to ethical considerations, results of continuous quality management (CQM) activities related to ethical performance, and patient records that may reflect transfers or progress notes on contact with extrahospital groups to be involved in patients' aftercare.

Table 1.2 lists the program responsibilities mentioned immediately above that are relevant to organizational ethics. Corresponding evidence of degree of meeting these responsibilities that surveyors might use is also listed there.

CHAPTER 2

Continuum of Care

Elizabeth D. Brown
Karen Boies-Hickman

The Joint Commission evaluates your continuum of care from the pre-entry phase, to the entry phase, to within the organization, to the pre-exit phase, and, finally, to the exit phase. This chapter addresses these stages and begins with a discussion on how we think about a continuum of care. In psychotherapeutic and psychoeducational programs, the key element is matching appropriate treatment resources with the assessed needs of patients. When addressing this match, your staff members evaluate what they need for patient care and what your treatment environment can provide. At different times in the treatment cycle, substance-abusing patients may need a medical detoxification or a rehabilitation program. Alternatively, they may need an aftercare program geared toward prevention of relapse or a different kind of aftercare program focused on some specialized issue. Being able to effect a good match is dependent on work previously done by your leadership. You must have successfully created or garnered the resources available for given levels of the continuum of care. Moreover, you must have imparted to your staff enough information to place patients appropriately. Proper orientation and teaching of staff leaves them knowing better how to plan for patients as they move forward, backward, or sideways through the continuum of care.

As noted in the flowchart shown in the *1995 Accreditation Manual for Mental Health, Chemical Dependency, and Mental Retardation/ Developmental Disabilities Services (MHM)* (Joint Commission, 1995, Vol. 2, Figure 2, p. 32), a systems-level planning process takes place before individuals can enter treatment. This planning provides the basis for policies and procedures designating how patients enter treatment and how they are assessed for treatment needs and required level of care. These planning documents also should specify how patients move through the system of care as a function of continued assessment and treatment planning. The documents describe patients' movement until they are transferred to another setting or service or discharged. The policy and procedure materials list criteria used by staff as they work with their patients in assessing ongoing care needs. Substance abuse patients should be active and informed participants in the process, a status acknowledged by material in policy and procedure documents.

This chapter generally follows the format established by the *MHM* (Joint Commission, 1995). As such, it begins with material on screening for admission and then moves to entry into care. It goes on to address the need to help patients to be knowledgeable in their decision making about entering care. Next, it shifts to the processes used to move informed patients from one level of care to another and from one clinical provider to another. These transitions may involve the discharge of patients or the transfer of their care to another care-providing agency. The chapter concludes with material related to handling instances in which patients in need of services are ruled ineligible for care reimbursement.

Screening and Initial Assessment (CC.1 and CC.2)

Decisions about the initial placement of patients in the continuum of care are based on screening and initial assessment, with the goal of maximizing the fit between patient needs and treatment resources. Thus, on patients' entry into your program, your assessment of their needs and your knowledge of the resources available to you will come together to determine the type and level of care needed.

Two sets of standards address how patients enter your continuum of care: CC.1 and CC.2. It is difficult to make a distinction between these two sets because they overlap. Therefore, this chapter treats CC.1 and CC.2 as one set of standards. We believe that our recommendations under one heading will bring you into compliance for both sets.

As stated above, the *MHM*'s continuing-care standards call for evidence that your program has developed and is using mechanisms for a timely and sufficient response to treatment requests. As noted earlier, you must define these mechanisms in a policy and procedure memorandum. You can describe the parts that make up the mechanism in addenda to the memorandum. Such addenda might include admissions criteria for your various levels of care, a description of the thoroughness of the screening procedure, and the methods for having screening done on an emergency basis. We suggest that you also specify exclusionary criteria for treatment entry. For instance, if a recently relapsed patient successfully completed your rehabilitation program, say, within the past 6 months, your criteria might exclude the option of another rehabilitation cycle. As another example, you might want to specify a certain period of time between inpatient admissions for detoxification. In developing a plan for your continuum of care, we recommend that you think about the strengths and weaknesses of the referral linkages. At one facility, some linkages may be well established: For example, an eligible intoxicated patient appearing at the hospital's emergency room may be admitted for detoxification provided that there is a bed available. Other linkages may still be at an exploratory stage: For example, how does the newly developing satellite program, 60 miles removed from the hospital proper, connect with the main-site detoxification program to get an intoxicated patient, who needs an inpatient level of care, admitted as an emergency case when no transportation is available? Attention to the quality of transfer will allow your staff to know where to put program development efforts to enhance continuity of care. Problems of weak linkages are critical areas for resolution in your strategic planning process. As you resolve problems such as these, you should establish a paper trail to include with your other materials for the surveyor.

Table 2.1 Standards Related to Entry Into Care and Evidence of Compliance

Standards	Evidence of Compliance
Mechanism for timely and initial contact (CC.1)	Admissions criteria, including adequate response to exclusionary criteria; policy and procedure
Evidence that the mechanism is implemented (CC.1)	Record review: utilization review data and reports; log showing referrals to other agencies for patients who fail to meet admission criteria
Entry into care based on assessment and transfer procedures (CC.2)	Intake policies and procedures; intake admission plans; staff interviews
Eligibility for services based on criteria (CC.2.1)	Policy and procedures; admissions criteria, including exclusionary criteria; clinical records; staff interviews; log showing referrals to other agencies for patients who fail to meet admission criteria

The mechanism itself is merely descriptive and prescriptive. Implementation is another matter and must be in place for an acceptable score. Be prepared to give examples of how your staff follows policy. For instance, you might want to show that you have a procedure for safe handling of an intoxicated patient who is refusing admission for detoxification. You might note that your admitting staff looks at the criteria for ambulatory care detoxification and for inpatient detoxification in deciding how to enter the patient into an appropriate level of care. You might show that a utilization review process takes place within, say, 48 to 72 hours after hospitalization to determine if the patient is at the correct level of care. You might point out that your admissions criteria consider heterogeneity in your patient population and thus are different for different subgroups of addicted patients. You might address how you handle dually diagnosed patients. Table 2.1 provides a summary of what surveyors will be looking at and ways that you can show that your program is in compliance.

Providing Information About Care Options (CC.3)

If you have not already done so, you need to develop materials and resources for informing newly admitted patients and their families about the care you plan to provide. Information about the nature and goals of care and the hours during which it is available should be listed in a brochure or other printed material that your staff gives to patients and their families. While you are interviewing the patient for intake or interviewing a patient whose sensorium has improved after sufficient detoxification, you should present all of this information. We suggest that you have patients repeat their understanding of the information you have provided. This activity not only gives you the chance to correct any misunderstandings but also may reinforce patients' memory about the information.

The *MHM* addresses information that you give to a patient about the costs he or she may have to bear. These costs may be related to a co-pay, a deductible, or the refusal of an insurance company or managed-care company to pay for certain types of treatment. (This last topic is treated later in this chapter.) Your staff need to know about alternate treatment options, either in your own continuum of care or in another agency, that can lighten the burden for patients who lack the financial resources for a costly course of treatment.

Although the *MHM* does not address Employee Assistance Plans (EAPs), the topic merits the attention of SATP leaders. Your program may or may not offer an intensive enough program to meet the needs of some employees. Sometimes agencies may limit assistance to a certain time period; often the EAP does not provide inpatient care, even if needed for detoxification. Exceptions to these limitations can be made if the employee is covered through insurance or through veteran eligibility in VA settings. We urge you to use the same guidelines in working with EAP patients as you do with other patients who need treatment but lack sufficient funds for payment. We say more about the treatment of EAP patients in Chapters 1 and 4 of this book. Chapter 1 discusses the ethical quandaries encountered when staff members seek treatment at a facility where they work and how that treatment might best be managed.

Your written materials, including brochures and handbooks, your intake process, and subsequent contact with patients are opportunities to address patients' involvement and rights and responsibilities in care. For instance, inpatients need to know that if they bring alcohol or drugs onto the agency's grounds, discharge will follow. We recommend that you inform court-mandated patients about the use of Breathalyzers and/or urine testing to show compliance with treatment. Table 2.2 lists elements covered under CC.3.

Table 2.2   Standards Related to Patients' Informed Decision Making in Entering
Care and Evidence of Compliance

Standards	Evidence of Compliance
Patients (and family members, when relevant) have information about the nature and goal of the care (CC.3.1)	Policies and procedures; clinical records; interviews with patients and significant others; posted material; patient handbooks; fliers and brochures; check-off list used in intake interviews (or when patient's sensorium is clear enough to allow interviewing)
Patients (and family members, when relevant) have information about the hours during which care is available (CC.3.2)	Interviews with patients and significant others; posted material; patient handbooks; fliers and brochures; check-off list used in intake interviews
Patients (and family members, when relevant) have information about the costs of care, if any, to be borne by them (CC.3.3)	Interviews with patients and significant others; data sheet delineating costs and sliding fee scale, if appropriate; check-off list used in intake interviews
Patients (and family members, when relevant) have information about their involvement and rights and responsibilities in the care (CC.3.4)	Policy and procedure; posted materials; patient handbooks, check-off list used in intake interviews; educational syllabi and attendance sheets
Patients (and family members, when relevant) have information about arranging for dependent care services, if necessary, during their involvement in care (CC.3.5)	Brochure addresses social worker assistance; intake document specifies whether assistance is needed

We also recommend that you provide staff with education and opportunities for discussion about what constitutes appropriate patients' responsibilities. We have found a basic disagreement among those staff members who want to call patients before appointments as a reminder and other staff who insist that remembering an appointment be the patient's responsibility. Your educational syllabi and staff meeting minutes relevant to this topic can be kept with the other materials for the surveyor.

In CC.3.5 the *MHM* has standards and examples of implementation for arranging for dependent care services, if necessary, while patients are receiving treatment. We have found that patients have had good experiences in leaving their children at an on-site child care program while seeing an outpatient provider. Similarly, we have had good experience with college student volunteers providing similar services for patients enrolled in evening programs. In both instances the child care has been on the grounds and provided either by licensed staff or in an observable waiting room. We are wary of the implementation example that the Joint Commission has given for maintaining a list of self-help group members willing to care for dependents and even to live at patients' homes during inpatient treatment. In this day of frequent reports of abuse by care providers and in today's litigious climate, we recommend that you broach this topic with any legal counsel available to you and with your risk manager. We encourage you to use the expertise of the social workers on your staff in developing acceptable resources for dependent care.

Continuity Over Time/Providers' Coordination (CC.4 and CC.5)

As patients progress through the care cycle, you need to engage in ongoing assessment of their needs, to continue to evaluate your treatment resources, and to maximize the match between patient needs and program resources. The success of the patients' progress through the continuum is dependent on constant communication: by staff with each other, by staff with patients and their families, and by staff with referring sources and aftercare agencies and groups. Your documentation in patient records should be clear on these points and obvious to surveyors. You also need background documentation describing the continuum of care, which may be part of the policy and procedure memorandum discussed earlier in this chapter.

With these various memoranda, you have a written plan showing the program resources and method of patient entry at the various points in the SATP system. This description also describes the functional relationships among your organization's parts. For example, at the micro-organizational level of one medical center, the leaders describe the SATP as a parent organizational unit that includes a number of component programs: a detoxification ward; an inpatient rehabilitation unit for the treatment of substance abuse; a longer stay inpatient rehabilitation unit geared toward the treatment of patients deemed to need the structure of a therapeutic community; an alcohol outpatient clinic at the medical center site; the Project for Counseling Alcoholic Marriages program (Project CALM); a Substance Use Post-Traumatic Stress Disorder (SUPT) program that is itself divided between the medical center site and another site some 60 miles away; and a newly developed outpatient detoxification/ rehabilitation program, also 60 miles removed from the medical center proper. The SATP leaders also describe the more obvious functional links among various programs: For example, detoxification is often followed by rehabilitation and/or standard outpatient care. Other links may be less obvious and raise questions whose answers may assist in more efficient programming and better patient care. For instance, the medical center staff has had to resolve the question of knowing whether a given patient who has completed the inpatient rehabilitation program best meets criteria for subsequent treatment in SUPT or in Project CALM.

You will want to show contracts/letters of agreement with external agencies to which you may refer patients whose treatment needs you can no longer meet. If your program has linkages with self-help groups such as Alcoholics Anonymous, you will want to have material specifying the nature of the connection. For example, if you provide free meeting space for current and past patients, you should have something saying when these meetings are held, if they are open to individuals whom you have never served, and so forth. If you use a case manager approach in working with patients, you may want to have a written description of the duties for your case managers. You may also list these duties in position descriptions and performance plans, as described in Chapter 9 of this book. For demonstration of compliance with the CC.5 standards, you may also want to have on hand schedules of regular team meetings, minutes from staff meetings, and any quality improvement data or reports that you have related to continuity of care. Table 2.3 lists standards and evidence of compliance in this area.

Referral, Transfer, or Discharge to Other Levels of Care (CC.6)

As a surveyor evaluates the adequacy of your transferring and referring practices, he or she will decide whether you have met the intent of CC.6. To get a score of 1, you must show a 91% to 100% compliance rate with all of the elements listed in Table 2.4. You might want to develop

Table 2.3   Standards Related to Movement Through the Continuum of Care and Evidence of Compliance

Standards	Evidence of Compliance
Continuity over time among the various phases of services (CC.4)	Policy and procedures; clinical records (treatment plans, new assessments, progress notes); staff interviews; evidence of a case manager approach
Coordination among the health professionals providing care (CC.5)	Policy and procedures; clinical records (progress notes, transfer/discharge summaries); staff interviews; evidence of a case manager approach; evidence of regular care team meetings

a template with space for addressing each of these items. Such an approach facilitates record reviews.

In demonstrating compliance with the transfer/referral standards, we recommend that you have on hand the following items: background materials, logs, contracts/letters of agreement, relevant minutes from team meetings or from your overall SATP organization's meetings, position descriptions (for case managers), and patient handbooks and brochures.

You should begin to establish discharge readiness criteria for the exit phase of a patient's care when you first write the comprehensive treatment plan and derive the objectives of treatment. We also address this topic later in Chapter 4 of this book. At that time, your team members assess which objectives are critical to the patient's ability to initiate a sober way of life outside of an inpatient program. In outpatient settings, staff members determine objectives for maintaining sobriety without the support of ongoing care. Once the team has identified critical objectives, it can use them to gauge patients' readiness for discharge or treatment termination: Specifically, once a patient has met all of the critical objectives, your staff knows that he or she is ready to move on. Table 2.5 lists discharge standards and evidence of compliance with them.

If team members do not use a process such as that delineated above, they may be vulnerable to making erroneous clinical judgments about patients' readiness to move to a new program in the continuum of care or to end treatment. Teams working in inpatient programs are susceptible to the risk of simplistically linking the completion of some set of

Table 2.4   Standards Related to Transfer/Referral in the Continuum of Care
and Evidence of Compliance (CC.6)

Standards	Evidence of Compliance
There is a mechanism for transfers.	Policy and procedure memoranda; staff interviews; clinical records; contracts; referral logs
The mechanism includes shifting of responsibility for the care of a patient from one clinician to another.	Policy and procedure memoranda; staff interviews; clinical records
The mechanism includes shifting of responsibility from one organization to another.	Policy and procedure memoranda; staff interviews; clinical records; referral logs; data on follow-up of patient
The mechanism includes shifting of responsibility from one organizational unit to another.	Policy and procedure memoranda; staff interviews; clinical records; minutes from meetings involving different units in your system of care; CQM information to show that problems unresolved from previous treatment remain designated in the care plan
The mechanism includes shifting of responsibility from one clinical service to another.	Clinical records; protocol for physician input in transfers to another service
There is a definition for when treatment will end and transfer will occur.	Policy and procedure memoranda; patient handbook; patient contracts; intake note
There are stated conditions under which transfer can occur.	Policy and procedure memoranda; patient handbook; patient contracts; contracts/ letters of agreement
Responsibility for the patient during transfer is not overlooked.	Policy and procedure memoranda; patient handbook; contracts/letters of agreement with external agencies
Mechanisms for referral/transfer can be through formal affiliations or in-formal arrangements by professional contracts.	Referral logs; contracts/letters of agree-ment with external agencies; clinical records

experiences, such as an educational program, with readiness for discharge. Teams easily recognize the extreme outliers, such as the homeless patient who needs to find a place to stay or the patient waiting for a bed in a halfway house. However, there is too often an assumption that most patients can leave at the end of, say, a 21-day program.

Table 2.5 Standards for Discharge From the Continuum of Care and Evidence of Compliance

Standards	Evidence of Compliance
Mechanism to identify patients who require discharge planning (CC.6.1)	Policies and procedures; contracts; clinical records; staff interviews
Informing patients in a timely fashion of the need for discharge/transfer (CC.6.1.1), including informing patients of the need for transfer to another organization or level of care, conveying this information in a timely manner, advising patients of any alternatives to transfer, telling patients of the reason for discharge in a reasonable time frame before the discharge date, and informing patients at the time of discharge how to continue to care for themselves.	Policies and procedures; copies of discharge/transfer instructions; materials given to patients; clinical records; check-off lists to show that all of the elements listed to the left in this table have been addressed

It is important that teams recognize that discharge is not a treatment event unique to inpatient settings but that it also extends to outpatient programming. In outpatient programs, there is a need for you to educate staff to write and use treatment objectives for treatment decisions, design plans for gradual end of treatment, develop follow-up mechanisms, and create an oversight function for ensuring that staff members carry out plans.

In keeping with its emphasis on good communication about shifts in treatment, the *MHM* addresses the need to inform patients fully and in a timely manner about any shift that will occur in their treatment. You need to meet the communication requirements delineated under CC.6.1.1. We suggest that you consider a template for filling in the information. Your staff can give a copy of the completed form to the patient and keep another copy in the clinical record. As mentioned earlier, having such information will make compliance evident.

Exchange of Appropriate Information (CC.7)

Because discharge plans also must address the post-exit phase of care (the period following discharge or referral to an external agency),

Table 2.6   Standards Related to Appropriate Communication in
Transfers/Referrals and Evidence of Compliance (CC.7)

Standards	*Evidence of Compliance*
The following communication elements have been covered: the reason for transfer or discharge; the individual's physical and psychosocial status at time of transfer; a summary of the care provided and progress toward achieving goals; and instruction and/or names of referrals provided to the individual	Clinical records; checked-off templates containing lists of elements in the left-hand column of this table

your treatment team must know the full range of disposition possibilities. They also must maintain open communication channels with placement sites, for three important reasons. First, such communication affords a way of following up on patients' progress. Second, such contact allows your staff to assess continually the quality of care at the follow-up site and the program's fit with patients. Third, a continuing dialogue allows the treatment team to know of planned changes in a program. Such knowledge can help in making decisions about the placement of patients in the future. It is not enough merely to inquire about care available at follow-up sites: A referral log listing the agencies to which patients are referred should be established and kept updated so that team members have accurate information for use in decision making.

The *MHM* addresses the need for communication from an additional perspective. The purpose of CC.7 is to ensure that you convey adequate information about the patient to the referral agency or transfer recipient. We list information that may be helpful in Table 2.6.

As discussed in more detail in Chapter 6 of this book, the Joint Commission mandates that you evaluate your discharge planning. To meet this standard, you can select an adequate sample of discharges and then obtain information for evaluation and documentation from accepting programs, agencies, and individuals. At some preset time post-discharge, you assign a staff member to send a form addressing the following points: patients' names, names of the persons contacted at the program, check-off options related to whether patients showed for their initial appointment and whether referrals were appropriate, and a space for writing any problems that the aftercare program had with the patient.

For more evidence of compliance with standards on appropriate communication in referrals, you can attach a copy of an uncompleted template to the form described above. The external agency can endorse check-off boxes showing whether the types of information it received was adequate for patient care. You would want to leave some space on this version of the template for comments about how your staff might improve in the way that they convey patient information.

Your staff member may need to make phone calls to minimize the problem of accepting agencies' failure to return follow-up requests. We suggest that you document the problems that you have discovered through the evaluation of the aftercare. Along with this documentation, you should include the plan of action for correcting the shortcomings. The results from your action plan should appear in minutes and CQM reports. You can demonstrate through subsequent discharge-planning efforts that you have resolved any communication problems in referring patients.

Mechanisms for Denial of Care Decisions (CC.8)

The final standard for continuing care relates to how you handle instances when reimbursement is not available for patient care. Such an event may be related to patients' lack of insurance, patients' inability to pay a deductible or co-pay, or the denial of reimbursement by a managed-care firm or insurance company. The intent of the CC.8 standard is that patients who present for and need care should be admitted to treatment even in the face of denial by a third-party payer. There are instances when care may be denied, but those cases must be ones in which law or regulation prohibits care. For example, only veterans who have gained eligibility status at the Department of Veterans Affairs can be treated at VA programs.

Your utilization review activity is important in negotiating with insurers or managed-care companies for the care of patients. You may want to adopt a commonly accepted method to validate the need for inpatient admissions. Although the use of InterQual standards is becoming widespread in many mental health programs, a method derived from the American Society for Addictions Medicine (ASAM) criteria may hold up better in inpatient substance abuse programs. In adapting such a set

Table 2.7   Standards Related to Handling Denial of Reimbursement for Care
Decisions and Evidence of Compliance

Standards	Evidence of Compliance
Implementation and performance of a mechanism to handle decisions to deny reimbursement for care, based on rulings of ineligibility (CC.8)	Policy and procedure; written material to show that each decision to show reimbursement for care is monitored by a patient utilization review care representative; external utilization review criteria available; written material to show that you have an appeals process; written code of ethics stating that care will not be withheld in cases in which care cannot be rendered legally; written instructions available to staff to make a referral; letters of agreement with potential recipients of referrals

of criteria, you also can use the utilization review results to assess the adequacy of your admission criteria and any subsequent changes in your admission criteria. Table 2.7 lists the standards for CC.8 and suggests some evidence you might want to produce to show compliance.

Summary

The multiplicity of programs in many SATPs and the complexity of treating substance abuse require considerable coordination in planning patient care. The objective is not only to attain the best treatment matching for patients as they go through a continuum of care but also to avoid cost inefficiency and redundancy. Without completion of the structural work of defining and describing the overall SATP and its parts, such coordination is not possible. Critical to the success of patients' movement through the continuum are the processes of ongoing assessment, continuing awareness of treatment resources, and communication characterized by quality and frequency. Chapter 2 has taken you through the processes of developing policy and procedure mechanisms for facilitating patients' movement through the entire cycle of care. We have addressed those points at which surveyors will expect to find evidence of implementation of policies and have provided suggestions for demonstrating compliance with all of the standards. Adequate communication among clinicians, among care sites, and with patients is an important factor in making progress through a continuous assessment/treatment cycle. Therefore we have included tables highlighting the essential components of these types of communication. We have concluded with a section on handling the care of patients who do not have the financial resources for treatment either because of a lack of funds or because of denial of reimbursement by a third-party payer. Throughout the chapter we have included references to other sections in the *MHM*. As we noted at the beginning of the chapter, standards may be written to represent what appear to be discrete units of the care process. But, in fact, care is a continuous and complex process that cannot be clearly broken down into units. For instance, assessment is not a solitary phenomenon; continuous assessment is needed to help patients to complete the care process successfully. Also, efforts at organizational improvement cannot be separated from the various aspects of the assessment and care processes. Because of the interwoven nature of the activities of interest in the accreditation process, we have given a wide range of examples to show not only that your program has defined what needs to be done but also that you have implemented and evaluated components in a manner congruent with the various standards.

CHAPTER 3

Assessment of Patients

John Gillick
Timothy J. O'Farrell
Elizabeth D. Brown
Karen Boies-Hickman
Robert J. Rotunda

Assessment occurs during the entire sequence of care. It begins when the patient first presents for services and extends to planning for discharge and aftercare. When surveyors evaluate the adequacy of the assessments of patients done in your program, they expect to see that qualified staff have gathered an array of appropriate data and used these data to plan and deliver individualized treatment. Moreover, surveyors look for evidence that your assessments demonstrate a continuing process that considers changes in the patient in response to treatment or to extra-program influences.

Joint Commission standards for assessment of patients are divided into four major areas:

1. Screening and assessment of patients (PE.1.1 to PE.1.15)
2. Additional requirements for assessment of specific patient populations, including individuals in chemical dependency programs (PE.1.16 to PE.1.18)
3. Assessment for discharge planning, care decisions, and reassessment (PE.1.19 to PE.3)
4. Structures supporting the assessment process (PE.4)

The first two areas of assessment specify in detail the information and procedures needed to assess each individual's physical and psychological status and social functioning. An assessment covering both areas has come to be known as a *biopsychosocial assessment*. The third area concerns uses that are made of the assessment data. The fourth area concerns the written policies and procedures about assessment that each substance abuse treatment program (SATP) must have. We shall consider each of these four areas in turn.

Screening and Assessment of Patients (PE.1.1 to PE.1.15)

Table 3.1 lists the key points we shall cover on Joint Commission requirements for screening and assessment. These requirements apply to all patients in mental health, substance abuse, and mental retardation/developmental disabilities programs. Later in this chapter we shall examine specific additional assessment requirements for patients in an SATP.

Initial Screening and Assessment (PE.1.1 to PE.1.4)

When an individual enters the SATP, staff must gather information to identify the reasons that brought the individual to treatment. On first contact with the patient, staff must screen and/or assess each individual's physical, psychological, and social status. The purpose of this initial biopsychosocial screening/assessment is to determine whether the individual needs SATP care and what particular type of care is needed. Staff also must identify areas that need further assessment.

Table 3.1 Key Points in Initial Screening and Assessment of Patients (PE.1.1 to PE.1.15)

Initial Screening (PE.1.1 to PE.1.4)
  Screen and/or assess each individual's physical, psychological, and social status to determine need for care, type of care, and need for further assessment.
  Assess for mental health problems that are life threatening, reveal severe personality disorganization, or may seriously affect treatment.
  Determine the need for assessing nutritional status.
  Determine the need for assessing functional status.

Clinical Assessments (PE.1.5 to PE.1.12)
  Emotional and behavioral assessment
  Psychosocial assessment
  Vocational and/or educational assessment
  Legal assessment
  Physical health assessment
  Diagnostic testing and waived testing

Determine What, If Any, Additional Assessments to Do (PE.1.13)
  Consider the organization's mission and scope.
  Consider the care setting and the individual's need and desire for care.
  Consider the individual's need and desire for care and response to previous care.

Assessment of Abuse and Neglect (PE.1.15)
  Develop and implement criteria to identify victims of alleged or suspected abuse or neglect.
  Assess victims of alleged or suspected abuse or neglect or refer to an appropriate setting for assessment.
  Assessment of victims of alleged or suspected abuse or neglect follows legal requirements for consent, for safeguarding evidentiary material, and for notification of proper authorities.

NOTE: Joint Commission standards also discuss assessment for anesthesia (PE.1.14) by an appropriately trained and licensed practitioner, including a preanesthesia and postanesthesia assessment. This book does not cover these standards, which do not apply to most SATPs.

Screen and/or Assess Each Individual's
Physical, Psychological, and Social Status (PE.1.1)

Each SATP must develop policies and procedures to define the scope and nature of the initial biopsychosocial screening/assessment. These written materials will vary considerably depending on the type of SATP and the patient population typically served by the SATP.

For example, Appendix B of this book contains an outline of information to be gathered for an intake screening note in a specialized spouse-involved outpatient program (described in detail in O'Farrell, 1993) that is part of a large SATP. Substance-abusing clients in this program typically are married or living with a partner and come to the initial interview after the substance abuser has completed detoxification. Note that staff gather specific information at the first contact about domestic violence and plans for separation or divorce because this information is crucial for determining whether staff need to pay immediate attention to these issues. Note also that staff in this particular program do not complete a comprehensive physical and mental screening at the initial contact. Often this type of screening has been done already during detoxification, and it generally is not needed to decide whether to schedule a second appointment for continued assessment and therapy.

Although each SATP has some latitude in defining the scope and nature of the initial biopsychosocial screening/assessment, the Joint Commission requires that certain items be included. SATP policy must address initial screening to determine when psychiatric evaluation and psychological testing need to be conducted. Further, the initial screening must specify the other areas that require further assessment. Finally, screening must assess for severe mental health problems and determine the need for assessing nutritional and functional status, each of which we briefly cover next.

Risk Assessment for Severe and Life-Threatening
Mental Health Problems (PE.1.2)

The initial screening should include a determination of the degree of the patient's danger to self or others, particularly in regard to the potential for a lethal act. Many patients in substance abuse programs have an elevated risk for suicide and/or violence. A thorough assessment of risk for suicide and homicide must be done at the start of each treatment episode and when any untoward incident occurs during treatment. Appendix B of this book contains a series of screening items to identify such problems. Continued careful assessment of the risk for suicidal and homicidal behavior, particularly at times of crisis or relapse among patients with a history of such behavior, is required for both clinical and risk management reasons.

Your staff also should identify mental health problems that may seriously affect the patient's ability to benefit from admission to an SATP.

For one, your staff members should assess the patient's motivation for treatment. If they find that an unwilling, mentally compromised, or mentally incompetent patient is brought in by a family member, your program may waste its resources in attempting treatment. More critically, the patient's impaired mental condition may preclude immediate treatment of his or her substance abuse. For instance, if the initial assessment reveals that a patient is in an acute stage of a psychiatric disorder, that patient probably should be stabilized in acute psychiatry before being transferred for substance abuse treatment. If a homeless, substance-abusing patient has pneumonia or some other medical disorder requiring acute intervention, that patient should be stabilized in a medical setting before treatment for substance abuse begins. Once staff have decided to offer treatment, they do a formal assessment to determine specific patient treatment needs.

Determine the Need for Assessing Nutritional Status (PE.1.3)

The initial screening and/or assessment should identify individuals who are at moderate or high nutritional risk so that a qualified dietitian can perform a nutritional assessment. Many substance-abusing patients face a significant nutritional risk in that they are malnourished owing to a poor quality of diet. In addition, many have serious medical conditions that mandate special attention to nutritional needs. Once identified, such patients should have an assessment and, when relevant, a care plan by a dietitian.

Determine the Need for Assessing Functional Status (PE.1.4 and PE.1.4.1)

The initial screening and/or assessment should identify individuals who may benefit from a functional assessment by a qualified rehabilitation professional. For example, it may be noted that a patient might benefit from physical rehabilitation for better recovery from, say, a fractured femur that occurred as a result of the patient's falling while inebriated. If the fracture has led to some loss of physical capacity, physical therapy may assist the patient in coming to a fuller recovery. Functional assessments may also be undertaken when patients are candidates for psychosocial or vocational rehabilitation programs. In these cases, the intent of the assessments is to determine if the patient has the skills, ability, and motivation to make good use of rehabilitative programs. Such programs may include compensated work therapy or intensive work preparation training through homeless domiciliaries or sheltered work-shops.

Timing of Initial Screening

The Joint Commission requires that a complete medical history and physical examination be performed and documented for each patient within 24 hours of admission to an inpatient hospital SATP. For other aspects of care, the Joint Commission expects your team to follow its own policy for timeliness throughout the cycle of substance abuse treatment. More is said on this topic in Chapter 7 of this book. In terms of clinical practice, your staff should be aware of and comply with the timeliness requirements specified in your program's policies. Assigning specific staff members to specific tasks and/or patients may promote accountability and better adherence to your SATP's standards for time-liness and completeness of assessments.

After staff members complete the initial screening and/or assess-ment and decide that the patient is appropriate for treatment in your SATP, they develop an initial treatment plan to meet immediate patient needs (described more in Chapter 4). Then staff members conduct a more thorough clinical assessment to develop an individualized comprehensive treatment plan.

Clinical Assessments (PE.1.5 to PE.1.12)

Emotional and Behavioral Assessment

The emotional and behavioral assessment includes the following (PE.1.5.1.1 to PE.1.5.1.7):

1. A history of emotional, behavioral, and substance abuse problems or treatment
2. Current emotional and behavioral functioning
3. Maladaptive or problem behaviors

4. When indicated, a psychiatric evaluation to determine current and past psychiatric abnormality

5. When indicated, a systematic mental status examination with special emphasis on immediate recall and recent and remote memory

6. When indicated, psychological assessments, including intellectual, projective, neuropsychological, and personality testing

7. When indicated, other functional evaluations of language, self-care, visual-motor, and cognitive functioning

For SATPs that serve the chronically and persistently mentally ill, the emotional and behavioral assessment also includes an evaluation of the community resources currently used by the individual (PE.1.5.2).

Some initial emotional and behavioral assessment findings may be misleading owing to patients' recent intoxication or use of medication to manage withdrawal symptoms. In particular, the assessment of depression can yield false positives for patients who have recently received large doses of benzodiazepines for detoxification purposes. Moreover, such medication affects cognitive functioning. Because the mental status examination must assess the patient's immediate recall and recent and remote memory, patients who have received such medication need to be reassessed if they demonstrate signs of cognitive impairment on initial screening.

Memory assessment results may have implications for treatment planning or for further assessment. For example, patients with difficulties in recent memory functioning should not be placed in treatment that is highly didactic in nature. Patients who show continued memory impairment on reassessment may require formal, in-depth neuropsychological testing. If program staff do not include a neuropsychologist competent to perform the needed testing, the program should identify some community resource for contracting neuropsychological assessments. Patients with histories of learning disabilities require a more complete assessment to determine whether treatment modifications are needed for full participation in treatment. In addition, some assessment of reading level is helpful because some patients have significant reading comprehension problems. Such patients have difficulty with treatment activities that include large amounts of reading material.

Psychiatric assessment includes a determination of current and past psychiatric abnormality. We urge caution in this part of the assessment.

The closer in time assessments are performed to substance misuse, the more likely it is that they falsely identify some patients as having an abnormality. In particular, problems with depressed mood, mood fluctuation, panic attacks, and other anxiety states can be byproducts of the substance abuse. When the initial assessment reveals what appears to be a psychiatric disorder, we suggest reassessment after the patient has been abstinent at least a few days. For example, the Beck Depression Inventory (BDI; Beck & Beamesderfer, 1974) often yields relatively high scores when patients are just completing detoxification that are simply related to the patient's report of bodily symptoms experienced during both depression and substance withdrawal. However, repeated assessment with the BDI a week after completion of detoxification usually yields a decrease in the symptoms endorsed. We are not suggesting that all findings of psychiatric symptoms are false positives. As noted earlier, some patients have comorbid affective or anxiety disorders. In fact, some patients use substances to medicate themselves for psychiatric disorders.

Emotional and behavioral assessment also should cover lifetime exposure to traumatic events. These occurrences include victimization by violent crime, domestic violence, rape and sexual abuse, childhood abuse, military combat, and other traumatic events. Patients with such experiences will need thorough evaluation for post-traumatic stress disorder (PTSD) and for understanding the role these events have played in initiating or maintaining the addiction.

Some programs have found it beneficial to use certain tests, instruments, and inventories in assessing psychological and cognitive functioning. Various tests have been used as cognitive screening devices: the Shipley Institute of Living Scale (Shipley, 1940), the Bender Visual Motor Gestalt Test (Bender, 1938), the Graham-Kendall Memory for Designs Test (Graham & Kendall, 1960), subtests of the revised version of the Wechsler Adult Intelligence Scale (WAIS-R; Wechsler, 1981), the Wechsler Memory Scale-Revised (Wechsler, 1987) and the Trail-Making Test from the Halstead-Reitan Neuropsychological Test Battery (Reitan & Wolfson, 1985). Personality assessment and assessment of psychological symptoms have been conducted through use of the Minnesota Multiphasic Personality Inventory (MMPI-2; Butcher, Dahlstrom, Graham, Tellegen, & Kaemmer, 1989), the Millon Clinical Multiaxial Inventory (MCMI; Millon, 1994), the BDI, and the State-Trait Anxiety Inventory (Spielberger, Gorusch, & Lushene, 1970). Some programs have used screening batteries composed of instruments such as the Shipley Institute of Living Scale, the Trail-Making Test, and the BDI and/or inventories that address issues important to the program. As noted earlier, the clinician must assess the mental clarity of patients before administering such screening batteries.

Psychosocial Assessment (PE.1.6 to PE.1.6.3)

Your SATP must define an effective psychosocial assessment based on the identified needs of your patient population and congruent with the methods of intake and admission described in your policies and procedures. The psychosocial assessment includes information related to the following topics, to the extent that you deem them necessary for your patients (PE.1.6.1.1 to PE.1.6.1.9):

1. Environment and home
2. Leisure and recreation
3. Religion
4. Childhood history
5. Military history
6. Financial status
7. The social, peer group, and environment setting from which the individual comes
8. Sexual orientation
9. The individual's family circumstances, including the constellation of the family group, the current living situation, and social, ethnic, cultural, emotional, and health factors

We shall review a few of the areas that sometimes present problems to staff in SATPs.

Leisure and recreation, including vocational interests and hobbies, are part of the psychosocial assessment. You can conduct this type of assessment at two different levels. If you have a licensed occupational therapist, a recreational therapist, or a vocational counseling specialist on staff, you do a comprehensive assessment. If you lack such staff, you still must address at least patients' previous and current recreational and leisure activities. These assessments are particularly valuable in programs with a social learning or relapse prevention focus in that the activities can be used as potential alternatives to substance abuse and as means to increase self-esteem through mastery. For example, some programs facilitate patients' earning their high school General Equivalency Diploma (GED) while in treatment. Success in doing so not only is a positive outcome for the patients but also improves their vocational prospects.

As part of this recreational and leisure assessment, we recommend that you ask patients to describe their daily activities in detail. Although patients may initially state that they are "doing nothing," it is important that your staff understand the pattern of daily activities. In particular, you can assess whether the patient's substance abuse occurs more frequently when alone or in the company of other substance abusers.

Military history, like other aspects of the psychosocial assessment, may be gathered in more or less detail depending on the SATP setting and patient population. For example, in VA settings where patients are military veterans and where there may be specialized therapy resources available for treating post-traumatic stress disorder, this aspect of the history may be more detailed than in other settings. In VA settings, such additional assessment requires taking a history of the patient's military experiences, including those that may have an impact on service-connected pension status and/or on rehabilitation potential. Relevant entries include dates of service; branch of service; location of service (noting war zone theaters, if applicable); the nature of any exposure to combat, including details of operations, overall length of exposure, the patient's reaction at the time of and since combat, and injuries received; whether the patient witnessed death, injury, mutilation, or torture; the nature of any prisoner-of-war status, including dates of capture, experience during incarceration, and conditions of rescue or repatriation; hospitalization during military service; whether there have been claims of exposure to herbicides or military nuclear ionizing radiation; whether there have been claims for a service-connected pension for post-traumatic stress disorder; whether medical care was rendered during active-duty status; and rehabilitation and employment potential.

Social, peer group, and cultural influences are also part of the psychosocial assessment. Your staff should assess the social and cultural influences on patients, including their values, beliefs, and spiritual orientation. In developing treatment plans, teams need to consider the following questions: Is this patient strongly identified with his or her cultural background? Is the cultural background one that supports the use of substances? Is the cultural group a minority in the geographic area? Are there cultural organizations that are potential affiliative resources for him or her? Are there Twelve Step group chapters composed primarily of persons from the same cultural background? Are there cultural holidays in which consumption of alcohol or other drugs is either tolerated or endorsed? Assessment also covers a patient's ability to participate with peers in programs and social activities. This ability can be assessed in several ways. Pertinent self-report information may be contained in patients' description of their leisure activities and involvement with others. In addition, staff can observe the patients' social behaviors in the therapeutic environment, especially in inpatient programs.

Sexual orientation and history are an important part of the psychosocial assessment. Staff need to get data about sexual orientation and sexual identity, particularly as these relate to patterns of substance abuse and to participation in SATP activities. In addressing the patient's sexual history, staff members seek information about histories of sexual abuse either as a victim or as a perpetrator. In the former case, knowledge of a patient's having been abused may influence how you design his or her treatment in that such abuse has been shown to be highly correlated with chemical dependence. In the latter case, your interviewer should assess whether high-risk sexual behaviors have occurred under the influence of substances. The sexual history must be taken at the assessment phase of the treatment cycle, even if staff members defer the actual treatment of sexual abuse until the patient has maintained abstinence. Staff also need to get data about sexual performance problems. Some patients are surprisingly unaware of the negative impact of substance use on sexual performance. Questions concerning sexual performance can be addressed during the physical examination.

Family participation is also addressed under the psychosocial assessment. The Joint Commission requires that the assessment include determining the need for participation of family members or significant others in the individual's care (PE.1.6.2). The intent is that family members should be considered at an early stage as potential sources of information about the patient and as resources in the treatment process. This standard is consistent with the growing body of research showing that involving family members in the assessment and treatment process for substance abusers leads to better treatment outcomes (O'Farrell, 1993; Peterson, Swindle, Phibbs, Recine, & Moos, 1994).

The patient's social support network, including family and peer relationships, and interviews with family members and significant others can provide invaluable information. Before contacting the family, staff should obtain permission from the patient to contact family members and should document the patient's consent in the patient's medical record. Then staff can interview the family members, preferably in person, but at least by telephone. Family members' interviews can be valuable even when the patient is not residing in the family home. Although the patient may give a great deal of information concerning the family, it often happens that recent substance abuse has led the patient to become alienated from family members and unaware of their activities and their feelings. The interviews may be good opportunities to link family members with Al-Anon or family support groups.

In addition to assessing family relationships, interviews should address the availability of friends and significant others as social supports. Support for patients' abstinence can come from surprising sources, including bartenders and former drinking friends. In some tightly knit communities, patients find that AA groups are composed of those friends. Other community groups in which the patient may be active, such as church groups or health clubs, may provide support for a healthier lifestyle.

Vocational and/or Educational Assessment (PE1.7)

Addressing vocational and educational issues is an important part of many patients' rehabilitation process. To develop a vocational plan, your staff members need to know a patient's educational level, vocational status, job performance history, vocational interests, and vocational aptitude. At times, you may want a standardized vocational aptitude test battery. In addition, exposure to a therapeutic work setting as part of an extended residential treatment program can help assess a patient's work habits and employment readiness. Qualified staff can compare vocational data to those from the psychological assessment to establish concordance among intelligence, educational level, and vocational status.

Including a vocational component in SATP programming is important because many substance abuse clients are underemployed given their educational level. The reverse situation also can be found and may be a factor in substances' being used to moderate job stress. In assessing the patient's job performance history, your staff should not only review the number and types of jobs patients have held but also determine any correlation between the type of employment and relapse. For example, some patients are most vulnerable to relapse when they are working out of town and away from their family support system. Other patients move from compulsive substance abuse to compulsive working and find themselves vulnerable to relapse unless working excessively. A steady job with regular hours that does not involve exposure to substances can boost self-esteem, occupy time formerly spent in substance use, and provide financial benefits. In addition, some jobs also provide a means for continued treatment through an EAP and other on-site recovery activities.

Legal Assessment (PE.1.8)

Assessment also includes gathering information about current and previous legal involvement and problems. These issues most frequently involve divorce, child custody, bankruptcy, and misdemeanor and criminal charges. Your staff members should determine whether the patient's legal problems have been primarily for drinking-related offenses, such as driving while intoxicated (DWI). Assessment also should evaluate whether offenses occurred under the influence of substances and whether any crimes were characterized by poor impulse control and violence. Your staff can use this last information to supplement the psychiatric/psychological assessment regarding judgment and the lethality assessment regarding problems with aggression. Further, patients' involvement in probation or parole needs to be assessed. If patients are active in either status at the time of the assessment, the probation/parole officer can be an important resource in treatment.

Physical Health Assessment (PE.1.9)

The assessment of physical health includes a comprehensive medical history and physical examination completed with attention to the problems characteristic of substance-abusing patients.

As such, the physical assessment must address the issues of the physical sequelae of substance abuse for the patient. These may include the acute effects of alcohol withdrawal, liver disease, malnutrition, neuropathies, cardiomyopathies, organic brain damage, and gastrointestinal disease such as pancreatitis, peptic ulcer, and colitis. Tests for communicable diseases address the increased rate of tuberculosis seen in the substance-abusing population, and, with patient permission, determine patients' HIV status. Careful history taking provides information on the extent of prior physical trauma, particularly head trauma, from falls, accidents, or assaults.

Diagnostic Testing and Waived
Testing (PE.1.12 to PE.1.12.3.3.2)

Generally, the patient's record should include the results of medical laboratory tests, such as common CBC and SMA-18 screening, completed as part of the physical assessment. In addition, the chart should contain appropriate laboratory screening tests, ordered on the basis of the findings of the history and physical examination. When a staff member anticipates having an interpretation of test results returned, the Joint Commission expects sufficient detail on the consultation request to allow the diagnostic question to be answered.

Pathology and clinical laboratory services needed for medical testing can be contracted to outside laboratories or conducted by those within your SATP or parent organization. If the laboratory services used by your program are considered to be of moderate or high complexity by federal guidelines (CLIA-88), they are accredited by the Joint Commission under the stipulations of the *Accreditation Manual for Pathology and Clinical Laboratory Services (LSM)* (Joint Commission, 1993). For your SATP to receive Joint Commission accreditation, the laboratory your program uses must meet the *LSM* standards.

The SATP program itself has direct responsibility for testing methods classified as "waived testing" under federal guidelines. These are tests for which the SATP defines the extent to which the test results are used in an individual's care (i.e., definitive or used only as a screen). Activities related to using a Breathalyzer or conducting urine drug screens fall under this set of standards. The Joint Commission expects that program policies and procedures exist to guide those staff doing such testing and that there is evidence in staff position descriptions of appropriate delineation of responsibilities. Moreover, your staff training records should show that education about alcohol and drug testing is part of new staff's orientation and regular continuing education. Additional evidence of sufficiently prepared staff may exist in CQM data and/or in staff minutes. Finally, any review of patient records must show that results from drug screens or from Breathalyzer applications have been done by qualified staff. More is said about staff qualifications for other types of assessment or intervention activity in Chapter 4 of this book.

Determine Which, If Any, Additional
Assessments to Do (PE.1.13)

Your staff should undertake assessments beyond the minimum Joint Commission requirements when warranted by the patient's diagnosis, when appropriate to the care setting, when deemed beneficial on the basis of the patient's desire for care, or when considered important on the basis of the patient's response to previous care. For example, if the patient's presentation suggests an affective or thought disorder, you might seek in-depth psychological testing. If physical assessment suggests some abnormality, the patient might be referred for additional specific tests such as a CAT scan or an evaluation by a neurologist or another medical specialist. Should a patient express interest in furthering his or her education, you might consider assessment by an educational specialist. If an inability to remember things critical to a patient's job performance is found, neurological examination and neuropsychological testing might be indicated.

Your staff may decide to gather additional assessment data compatible with specific elements of your program's treatment components. As a case in point, you may want to expand your assessments to be compatible with the orientation of your program (family therapy, cognitive-behavioral, relapse prevention) or special patient groups that you treat (geriatric, mentally ill chemical-abusing [MICA], PTSD). As such, if your outpatient program has a strong family therapy emphasis, you might include a genogram as part of the family history. Similarly, if you treat MICA patients, you may require a more comprehensive psychiatric assessment, including a review of the psychotropic medication.

Assessment and Reporting of Suspected
Abuse or Neglect (PE.1.15)

The Joint Commission requires that your assessment staff be sensitive to findings that may be consistent with abuse, including physical assaults, domestic abuse, sexual abuse, and abuse of elders or children.

Written policies and procedures should describe how staff members are to conduct the assessment of possible abuse. Further, these materials should specify the informed consent procedures to be used and reporting mechanisms required by law. Any clinical record in which the question of alleged or suspected abuse or neglect is raised should have progress notes that demonstrate that staff members have taken appropriate action in reporting the abuse. When formulating criteria for handling the assessment of abuse and its reporting, your staff should be aware of local law. Staff education about the assessment and reporting of abuse should be part of staff members' orientation and part of your ongoing staff education program.

In addition to getting informed consent from victim patients, your staff should be able to inform patients about any possible infringements on the privacy of their reports. For example, at the time of this writing, if a woman substance abuser seeks rape counseling services at a community clinic in Massachusetts, her records can be subpoenaed by attorneys representing the alleged perpetrator of the abuse for use in his defense. Staff should know how such local rulings may affect the privacy of records so that the patients can be duly informed.

Questioning whether abuse or neglect has occurred can produce a positive outcome. For example, the 14-year-old stepdaughter of a male patient in an inpatient SATP hinted at school that she was being abused. A meeting with the family revealed that the girl was reacting to a recent television show and that no abuse had occurred. The family meeting also revealed that a 16-year-old in the family was pregnant for the second time. Her first-born child was being reared within the family, with chief responsibility assumed by the wife of the SATP inpatient. This mother/grandmother was very upset about the second pregnancy and had refused to arrange medical care for her pregnant daughter. When staff questioned whether the teenager was the victim of reportable neglect, the family arranged for obstetrical care. They also agreed to outpatient family therapy that led to reduced family turmoil and a more supportive environment for the husband's recovery.

Table 3.2 displays the main areas we have addressed regarding initial screening and assessment of patients. It also outlines major sources of evaluation that the Joint Commission surveyor may examine to determine the extent of your SATP's compliance with these standards

Table 3.2   Standards for Initial Screening and Assessment of Patients and
Evidence of Compliance (PE.1.1 to PE.1.15)

Standards	*Evidence of Compliance*
Initial screening (PE.1.1 to PE.1.4)	Policy and procedures manual Clinical records Written plan for clinical services
Clinical assessments (PE.1.5 to PE.1.12)[a]	Clinical records Policy and procedures manual Written plan for clinical services Clinical staff bylaws, rules, and regulations
Determine what, if any, additional assessments to do (PE.1.13)	Policy and procedures manual
Assessment of abuse and neglect (PE.1.15)	Clinical records

a. The laboratory diagnostic testing and waived testing standards that are part of clinical assessments have other sources of evaluation. These include interviews with the laboratory director, a copy of the lab's letter of certification or accreditation, and interviews with clinical staff regarding their perceptions of the adequacy of lab services. For waived services such as collecting specimens for drug abuse urine screening or use of a Breathalyzer for alcohol intoxication, evidence includes review of documents showing staff orientation and competence assessment for conducting these procedures.

that apply to all patients. Next, we turn to some additional requirements for specific patient populations.

Requirements for Specific Patient Populations (PE.1.16 to PE.1.18)

The Joint Commission has additional assessment requirements for children and adolescents, for patients in chemical dependency programs, and for individuals with mental retardation/developmental disabilities. We next consider the first two of these categories.

Special Assessment of Children and Adolescents (PE.1.16)

SATPs for substance-abusing adolescents need to examine this standard carefully. Briefly, the Joint Commission *requires* the active participation of family members or the legal guardian throughout the assess-

Table 3.3   Additional Requirements for Assessment of Individuals in Chemical Dependency Programs and Services (PE.1.18)

A history of the use of alcohol or other drugs, including age of onset, duration, patterns, and consequences of use (PE.1.18.1)

The history of physical problems associated with dependence (PE.1.18.2)

Use of alcohol and other drugs by family members (PE.1.18.3)

Spiritual orientation (PE.1.18.4)

Types of previous treatment and response to that treatment (PE.1.18.5)

Any history of abuse, including physical or sexual abuse (as either the abuser or the abused) (PE.1.18.6)

ment and treatment process. The SATP must establish routine procedures to ensure ongoing communication with families or legal guardians. When adult patients are involved, your staff determine whether there is a need for family involvement in a patient's care, but for adolescent SATP patients, family involvement is required in each patient's care.

Special Assessment of Individuals in Chemical Dependency
Programs (PE.1.18)

The Joint Commission requires that the assessment of individuals receiving treatment for alcoholism or other drug dependencies specifically include the additional items noted in Table 3.3. We describe each of these next.

Substance Abuse History (PE.1.18.1)

Staff must compile a substance abuse history that provides information about the use of alcohol and other drugs, including age of onset, duration, patterns, consequences of use, and the types of and responses to previous treatment. So that the assessment is thorough, you may standardize the assessment to ensure that all forms of substance use in all patients are addressed. If only unstructured clinical interviews are used for such assessments, "clinical intuition" may lead practitioners to refrain from asking about certain forms of substance abuse. For example, a 60-year-old wealthy white male, widowed and living with a housekeeper, was initially asked only about his use of alcohol. On further examination, the assessor discovered that the patient had engaged in relatively recent assaults in taverns. A subsequent detailed assessment of his substance use found current use of marijuana and recent experimentation with cocaine. In fact, the cocaine usage was associated with the violence. The patient had been introduced to both substances by his housekeeper. Thus we recommend that you ask all patients about all forms of substance use, both current and by history.

An assessment is not clinically sound if it is based on erroneous data, an example of which may be underreporting of substance abuse. This type of reporting may occur for many reasons. For example, some patients consider marijuana to be an "herb," not a drug. Other patients may not initially endorse their use of benzodiazepines as potential substances of abuse, especially if they have been prescribed. It follows, then, that the assessment must address the use of medications, including those obtained over the counter, those procured through prescription, and those purchased illegally or borrowed from family and friends. As another example of underreporting, abusers of street drugs may minimize their reports of use of alcohol because they do not classify alcohol as a drug. Finally, commonplace examples of underreporting are uses of nicotine and caffeine. Alcohol-dependent patients have been known to consume up to 40 cups of coffee daily. If that use is not known, such patients can present confusing clinical pictures when either withdrawing from caffeine or using the same amount while in treatment.

The Addiction Severity Index (ASI) (McLellan et al., 1985) is a popular method for conducting standardized interview-based assessments. The ASI provides a structured method for interviewing the patient about current and previous use of substance use. It also assesses the extent of current problems in multiple areas (e.g., medical, occupational, family) and whether the patient wants help with these problems. Some programs have utilized the Michigan Alcoholism Screening Test (MAST) (Selzer, 1979) as part of a screening battery. In inpatient settings, the MAST has limited value because most patients admitted have significant dependence problems and score high on the MAST. The Alcohol Use Inventory-Revised (AUI) (Wanberg & Horn, 1983) can aid treatment planning in that it helps to identify what the patient sees as the benefits and consequences of drinking behavior.

In assessing the use of substances other than alcohol, we advise that the route of administration be determined. In cocaine usage, in particular, staff need to know whether the drug was snorted, injected intravenously, or smoked in its freebase form. Most patients report greater dependence resulting when cocaine is "freebased." Use of heroin also needs to be assessed as to whether it was injected or snorted. For patients who use more than one substance, the clinician should assess the patient's preferred drug or combination of drugs, as well as the responses to preferred and nonpreferred drugs. Information on this last topic is useful in treating those patients who experience idiosyncratic and even paradoxical reactions to substances.

Contradictions about basic information gathered from the patient are common in medical records of substance-abusing patients. Such discrepancies occur for a variety of reasons. For instance, a patient may cite one pattern of substance consumption during the nursing assessment at admission and report a different pattern during the psychological assessment 2 days later. The reports may differ as a result of a clearing of the patient's sensorium or because family members reminded the patient of drinking behavior in between sessions. Though it is understandable that these discrepancies occur, we advise that your team note and resolve them in the record. To facilitate this resolution, assessment information must be not only recorded but reported. Your team members must share information throughout the assessment process to plan adequate treatment for the patient.

Denial of excessive drinking and its social impact is a common phenomenon in substance-abusing populations. A patient's perception of his or her dependence may be used to undercut the denial. The ASI is a useful tool in acquiring this assessment information because it asks patients to assess the severity of their problems in all areas, specifically including their dependence. Family members can also report on how the substance abuse has affected the social network. For example, one patient in an inpatient alcoholism program was preoccupied with confidentiality and sought assurance that neither friends nor neighbors would find out about his problem. Family members later reported that the patient regularly fell asleep on the front lawn after becoming intoxicated at the corner tavern. The patient's focus on confidentiality decreased after this interview.

History of Physical Problems Associated
With Dependence (PE.1.18.2)

The history of physical problems related to substance abuse is another important topic. For example, a long recovery period following a DWI automobile accident may have produced considerable physical pain, a period of immobilization, economic hardship, social losses, and the need for intensive rehabilitation. The medical history and physical examination may find acute and chronic medical problems associated with dependence (e.g., liver disease, pancreatitis), substance-related physical trauma, and other such problems.

Use of Alcohol and Other Drugs
by Family Members (PE.1.18.3)

Data should be obtained about the use of alcohol and other drugs by a patient's family members. This history addresses not only the family of origin and family of procreation but also other close relatives or caretakers (honorary relatives or babysitters). As part of this history, the clinician explores the family history of participation and success in chemical dependence treatment. As a result of this assessment, your team should gain a basic understanding of the family dynamics regarding chemical dependence, the relative standing of the client in reference to the chemical dependence within the family, and the identification of potential family resources or role models for recovery.

Spiritual Orientation (PE.1.18.4)

Assessment of spiritual orientation is particularly important for substance abusers. The spiritual assessment does not focus solely on the patient's religious affiliation or activities. Twelve Step groups, which are often major interventions in SATPs, frequently have a strong spiritual focus. Assessment can help determine how comfortable the patient may be in such groups. Patients with little spiritual orientation may require extra assistance if they are to participate actively in such groups. For example, Alcoholics Anonymous and the Hazelden Corporation have published pamphlets for self-identified atheists or agnostics that address how they can participate in a group and still retain their values. Other resources include secular sobriety self-help groups such as Rational Recovery and

Secular Organization for Sobriety (S.O.S.). On the other hand, patients with a strong spiritual orientation may benefit from extra attention from a chaplain, priest, minister, rabbi, or some other religious person.

Types of and Responses to Previous
Treatment (PE.1.18.5)

Information concerning previous treatment can be valuable in designing current treatment for patients. In some cases, patients and practitioners minimize the importance of prior treatment experiences, almost as though they are invalid because relapse occurred. However, knowing where your patients have had previous treatment, whether it was completed, and how long they either remained abstinent or reduced usage after completing treatment can be useful in planning the current treatment phase. To make maximal use of such information, your staff should ask patients what they felt were the most and least helpful aspects of previous treatment. Staff should also ascertain what is different during the current course of treatment that might produce a better outcome.

History of Physical Abuse (PE.1.18.6)

Staff should inquire about any history of physical abuse, either as perpetrator or as victim. Information from family members can counter patients' tendency to under-report such problems. In particular, problems related to violence tend to be endorsed more often and in greater detail by family members. The special care for appropriate handling of this sensitive material and for complying with ethical and legal requirements when the patient is a perpetrator of abuse has already been covered in this chapter (above under PE.1.15).

Discharge Planning, Care Decisions, and Reassessment (PE.1.19 to PE.3)

Discharge Planning (PE.1.19)

Discharge planning should begin at the onset of inpatient admission. This planning should not be a one-time event. Rather, as your staff gain familiarity with individual patients, assess their progress through the program, and think about their posthospitalization treatment and residence needs, plans may take on new form or gain in complexity. Such alterations of discharge planning are most likely to emerge at the time of writing the comprehensive treatment plan after the comprehensive bio-psychosocial clinical assessment has been completed with the patient and, if appropriate, with family members.

Care Decisions (PE.2 and PE.2.1)

The Joint Commission requires that the many pieces of information gathered by various disciplines during the assessment process be analyzed and integrated by your team. In this way, the team can identify and prioritize the patient's needs that will be addressed during a specific episode of care. An integrated summary, often called a *diagnostic summary* or *formulation of the case*, provides a method for integrating data from various interdisciplinary team members during the process of treatment planning. The diagnostic summary is less detailed than individualized assessments but sufficiently comprehensive to stand alone as a review document. Importantly, it contains a problem list, which is the nucleus around which you formulate the patient's treatment. Your staff members should include information about the patient's strengths in the diagnostic summary. They may find some material relevant to this topic in patient interviews. Other potentially valuable information may come from self-evaluations written when the patient has more time for reflection. Appendix C of this book provides a sample diagnostic summary to illustrate the role this document plays as the midpoint between the assessment process and the treatment planning process, itself described in detail in the next chapter.

The diagnostic summary flows from a meaningful integration process in which your staff members have efficiently synthesized assessment information. The document should go beyond simplistically stated data to include a consideration of the meaning of the assessment for guiding the patient's treatment process. For instance, if a patient is found to have diabetes mellitus that is thought to respond to a particular dietary program, the patient's treatment plan should reflect that fact. If a patient is found to have an attention deficit disorder that could be minimized by presentation of educational material in some particular way, the treatment team should use this information in planning treatment. Other examples show how assessment data are mere facts unless they are dynamically integrated into the treatment process. Little is gained from learning that a person is of a certain ethnicity, but treatment can be enhanced by knowing how the patient's ethnic background affects his or her perceptions of substance abuse. Knowing a person's religious preference provides little, but knowing how the individual evaluates his or her substance abuse on the basis of his or her religious beliefs can help formulate an individualized treatment approach. There is little advantage in listing a patient's occupation, but information about how it interacts with the problem of substance abuse may be of great importance.

Reassessment (PE.3)

Joint Commission standards on assessment stipulate the need for reassessment of patients. You should specify the timing for formal reassessments in the memorandum or policy statement that establishes your program's expectations. These reassessments help determine how your patients are responding to treatment, how they are being affected by changes in their condition, and how their treatment should be altered because of a change in diagnosis.

Because treatment plan reviews are usually done at specified intervals, we recommend that you correlate them with the scheduled reassessments. These formal reviews are prescheduled events in which thoughtful and thorough evaluations of all interventions that have been used with a patient take place. If reassessment shows the need for treatment plan change, you update the treatment plan so that it reflects the new directions for treatment. Reassessment may also occur in informal reviews. For example, you may discuss a patient at a change-of-shift report or in a team meeting in which an entire roster of patients may be quickly reviewed.

Your program's policy and procedures determine the frequency of formal reassessment and reviews and often vary depending on the length and intensity of care available in the treatment program. A detailed progress note in the patient's record documents a reassessment and contains not only the current treatment goals but also the reassessment of patients' needs. When writing the reassessment progress note, your staff may consider six patient dimensions that may be relevant to patients at different points in their course of treatment:

1. Acute intoxication and/or withdrawal
2. Biomedical conditions and complications
3. Emotional/behavioral conditions and complications
4. Treatment acceptance/resistance
5. Relapse potential
6. Recovery environment

Under each heading the particular problems (listed by number) can be enumerated, the treatment reviewed, and the patient's progress or lack thereof documented. The note may continue until you exhaust the problems and relevant dimensions.

Patients need a revised treatment plan when

1. Some significant change within them or within their life has occurred.
2. The treatment previously selected now appears to be less effective than an alternative.
3. Errors in the assessment process have led to the development of an inappropriate plan for treatment.
4. Programmatic changes in the treatment delivery system have had a pronounced effect on patient care.

Changes in individuals or in their life conditions are easy to understand and are usually dealt with in practice. If a patient is diagnosed with a serious health problem or is faced with divorce, or if his or her child is arrested for a serious crime, we clinicians are attuned to how the patient's substance abuse treatment may be affected. It is important to alter treatment intervention and to reflect the change in modifications to the treatment plan. In addition, it is also important for us to assess how changes in what we have to offer may affect the patients' motivation and drive toward recovery. For example, how does the person being treated in an outpatient program interpret changes in clinic hours that will force him or her to lose time at work for a clinic appointment? Such changes may mean that something about the patient's treatment plan needs to be revised. Minor changes may be handled through a progress note: for example, group treatment changes to two 90-minute sessions a week rather than the three hour-long sessions stipulated by the treatment plan.

Structures Supporting the Assessment Process (PE.4)

The Joint Commission requires that the activities that constitute the assessment process be defined in writing. This requirement means that you have defined, in written policies and procedures, the role, scope, and content of each professional discipline's assessment. This definition must take into account the different settings in which care is provided as well as applicable state licensure and certification laws. So you must stipulate, for each part of the assessment process, who can and should carry out assessment activities. The Joint Commission specifies that a licensed independent practitioner must be responsible for care provided to any patient in an emergency care area (PE.4.2). The Joint Commission further specifies that a registered nurse must assess the patient's need for nursing care in all acute settings in which nursing care is provided (PE.4.3).

Summary

This chapter has described an extensive process of assessing what patients bring into treatment, what needs they have, and what you must do to demonstrate that assessment has been completed in a manner that is adequate, timely, and ethical. Three key points emerge from this material. First, assessment is not a one-time process. Rather, it is a necessarily recurring exercise to allow your staff to make maximal fit between the most current patient needs and the available treatment options. Second, assessment is a holistic undertaking and must consider all realms of a patient's functioning, including the environment in which he or she is to live and work when not in treatment. Third, assessment needs must be congruent with good clinical practice and with stated requirements that your organization has developed.

CHAPTER 4

Care of Patients

Elizabeth D. Brown
Timothy J. O'Farrell
Stephen A. Maisto
Margot G. Savage
Karen Boies-Hickman

The Joint Commission requires that the formulation of goals and services for each patient's care, treatment, and rehabilitation be individualized and appropriate to his or her severity level. This requirement does not mean that all of your patients must have individual psychotherapy. Rather, whatever intervention you decide on must be consistent with the needs of individual patients. If your program routinely discharges patients after they have finished a rehabilitation program of, say, 20 classes, you are probably not meeting the individualized treatment requirement. What you need instead are various treatment options that you can match with the assessed needs of each patient. For example, Mary Green's treatment plan may include individual therapy with a social worker to begin work on improving her self-esteem, group therapy led by a psychologist to help her with assertiveness, and classes selected from the general rehabilitative educational curriculum based on another need. Whatever treatment you provide, you should document it in progress notes according to your SATP's policy.

Joint Commission standards for care of patients are divided into five major areas:

1. Treatment planning (TX.1 to TX.1.21.6)
2. Medication use (TX.3 to TX.3.4.1)
3. Nutrition care (TX.4 to TX.4.6)
4. Rehabilitation care and services (TX.5 to TX.5.5.6)
5. Special treatment procedures (TX.6 to TX.6.6.5)[1]

The bulk of this chapter covers two main topics. First, we present an in-depth examination of what makes up good treatment planning. We emphasize treatment planning and documentation because they are more difficult for many staff members to master than the actual provision of services. The second major topic is the delivery of individualized services to patients. We also cover briefly the other topics addressed by Joint Commission standards about care of patients.

Treatment Planning

Individualized Care, Treatment, and Rehabilitation Goals

Table 4.1 lists the key points in the Joint Commission treatment planning standards. The first phase in the treatment planning cycle, the preliminary treatment plan, is the least complicated. Generally one staff member assesses the patient and prepares this first guide to treatment. This staff member often is the physician or registered nurse for inpatient admissions and an appropriately credentialed intake therapist for patients entering an outpatient program. This plan must be completed quickly (e.g., within 8 hours of an inpatient admission). Although the preliminary or initial treatment plan is critical in that it allows for

Table 4.1   Key Points for Treatment Planning in Care of Patients

Begin Treatment Planning Process (TX.1 TO TX.1.4)
  Individualize the plan.
  Formulate a preliminary plan after screening.
  Ensure that qualified, interdisciplinary staff members collaborate to plan and
    provide care.
  Ensure that the plan reflects the SATP's philosophy and participation from
    appropriate disciplines.
  Address emergent or immediate patient needs before completing the plan.

Treatment Plan Reflects Individual's Needs, Strengths, and Limitations
(TX.1.5 to TX.1.5.4)
  Document justification when a clinical problem is not addressed.
  Document the patient's and family's perception of the patient's needs.
  Document patient participation in developing the plan.
  Specify a plan for involving family or significant others when indicated.

Goals and Objectives for the Treatment Plan (TX.1.6 to TX.1.7)
  Formulate specific goals for the patient based on assessments of the patient and
    his or her family.
  Formulate specific objectives related to goals identified in assessment.
  Phrase objectives in measurable, behavioral terms with a projected date of
    achievement.

Treatment Plan Specifies Settings, Services, or Programs (TX.1.8 to TX.1.9)
  Base the plan on identified needs and specific goals and objectives.
  Include referrals for needed services that the SATP does not provide directly.
  Specify the frequency of treatment procedures.

Evaluate Care Against Goals and Make Plan Revisions (TX.1.10 to TX.1.11)
  Revise the plan when major clinical changes occur.
  Evaluate care at specified regular times.
  Specify criteria for termination of treatment.

Special Considerations (TX.1.12 to TX.1.14)
  Advance directives
  Oral health care needs in inpatient and residential SATPs
  Educational services for children and adolescents

NOTE: Treatment planning standards TX.1.15 to TX.1.21 address issues for mentally retarded/
developmentally delayed individuals that are not relevant to most SATPs.

individualized patient treatment to begin, this plan has a short life span.
You should replace it when the team is prepared to formulate the
comprehensive treatment plan.

When the entire interdisciplinary team has completed the assessments and formulated a diagnostic summary, the team is ready to

construct the comprehensive treatment plan. Some programs may believe that one staff member can develop the comprehensive plan by having access, through the diagnostic summary, to a multidisciplinary way of viewing each patient. We believe that having one staff member use assessment data from multidisciplinary sources to write a plan precludes the richness of a holistic discussion among team members about patients and their needs. Instead, we advocate an interdisciplinary approach in which staff members interact as a group in creating a plan. We believe such a plan will be more comprehensive and effective than a plan created by one staff member.

Time allowed for the completion of the comprehensive treatment plan varies depending on the type of program in which the treatment takes place. For example, the comprehensive plan might have to be completed within 3 days of admission to a brief-stay detoxification unit. On the other hand, it might take several sessions, spaced over several weeks, to gather enough data to write a meaningful comprehensive treatment plan for a patient who starts treatment directly in an outpatient SATP clinic.

What goes into comprehensive planning for individualized treatment? Although such planning may seem uncomplicated, your team must develop a number of skills to master the treatment planning process. Treatment plan writing requires that staff

1. Use the diagnostic summary to identify the many treatment needs inherent in the complex problems associated with each patient's substance dependence
2. Design a program of intervention tailored to the needs of that individual patient
3. Develop treatment objectives that are reasonable, attainable, and written in measurable and objective terms
4. Determine patients' goals for treatment and involve patients in developing their own treatment plan

In a rehabilitation program, these goals and objectives should address living, learning, and work activities beyond the goals and objectives related to gaining and maintaining sobriety.

Moreover, inpatient program staff must work toward an appropriate outpatient disposition that will continue the treatment begun in the inpatient setting. This requires that your inpatient staff be aware of and have access to postdischarge treatment options that are essential to the continuity of care required for a chronic disorder. Formulating a comprehensive treatment plan is a complex process. Before writing the plan, the team must come together to discuss the assessment findings and to evaluate which available treatment resources will be most helpful to the patient. We now move on to an outline for conducting these analyses.

Stating the Individualized Problem

When developing comprehensive treatment plans, your team looks at the individual patient's needs and goals for treatment, determines the individualized treatment services available to address these needs, sets individualized treatment goals and objectives, and establishes criteria for discharge. Once the team members have examined the patient's problem areas, they must decide which problems will be the immediate foci for intervention. The solution is "any within the capability of the team to address." Certainly, any area closely related to a patient's capacity for abstinence or physical health is very important. Your team also needs to ask which problems, if any, are beyond the team's capacity to handle and must wait until later in treatment or be referred outside the SATP for concurrent treatment. If you defer problems or consider them not amenable to treatment, enter a progress note explaining the rationale for the decision. Throughout the process, your team should consider the strengths that a particular patient brings to his or her treatment so that these strengths can be capitalized on in selecting treatment goals and activities.

Identifying the Settings and Services Required to Meet Goals

The second group of questions focuses on the resources available that staff members can use to help this patient:

1. Exactly how will we try to effect changes in the patient's behaviors and/or cognitions?
2. What are the strengths of our program that will best fit with the patient's needs, reinforce his or her strengths, and recognize his or her weaknesses?

3. If a critical part of our program is not acceptable for or to this patient, what can be substituted?

4. With what frequency and intensity should interventions occur?

5. Who within our team will be responsible for maintaining and evaluating the patient's progress?

6. Is a referral necessary for services not available within our team itself?

7. If referral is necessary, what is its nature? Is consultation enough, or does the "expert" need to take on the role of a temporary team member?

For example, if a patient had a childhood diagnosis of attention deficit disorder and currently appears to have a short attention span, might a neuropsychologist sit with the team for treatment planning to design the intervention most likely to hold the patient's attention? Planning for patients should extend beyond their stay in the SATP and should include services integrated with the community. Here staff members have to consider self-help groups and halfway or quarterway houses.

Writing Problem Statements for the
Comprehensive Treatment Plan

With answers to the questions about both patient needs and program resources, your team can turn to the actual writing of the comprehensive treatment plan. Start the process by stating the problem in the comprehensive treatment plan in clear, simple language free of professional jargon. The problem must be individualized to the patient and understandable by both patients and professional staff. These requirements are important in working with substance-abusing patients in that the comprehensive treatment plan usually will accompany the patient through more than one program in your continuum of care. As such, treatment staff in programs other than that where the plan was first formulated will need to understand the treatment issues. As an example of appropriate wording of a problem, the following may be considered. A male patient (whom we shall call John Coe) maintains that the main cause of his substance abuse is daily stress caused by frequent fighting with his wife and his teenaged children at home. In previous times, some staff might have listed such a problem as "denial" or perhaps as "marital and family problems." However, those descriptions do not yield an understanding of the individual patient or the exact nature of the problem. Consider the improvement in the following problem statement: "Patient's difficulty with assertiveness, related to observing parental role models who failed to resolve their own conflicts, and his trouble communicating effectively with his spouse and children contribute to family stress."

Qualified Individuals Plan for Treatment and Rehabilitation

Surveyors want evidence that you have carefully reviewed the qualifications of clinical staff members who plan and provide patients' treatment. We advise you to be prepared with credentialing folders (including performance ratings and continuing-education credits), peer review reports, quality management data, minutes from meetings of the SATP's credentialing committee, and any other information that shows that staff credentials and experiences are carefully reviewed. If the department (e.g., nursing, medicine) level decides basic staff qualifications, you can direct surveyors with questions there or to the quality assurance department. The SATP is responsible for qualifications related to experience and knowledge of substance abuse assessment, treatment, and rehabilitation. Chapter 9 of this book discusses procedures for determining and documenting staff qualifications in greater depth.

Evaluating Care Against the Goals and Making Treatment Plan Revisions

As stressed earlier, you will need to make a reassessment of each patient's goals and progress as the patient moves through your continuum of services. One efficient way to accomplish this is to give each problem listed in a patient's treatment plan a problem number and a short problem name. Then you can use corresponding problem numbers and problem names in writing problem-oriented progress notes. With this method, record reviewers can see quickly just which problem you are addressing at any particular point in the patient's chart.

Writing Goals and Objectives for the Comprehensive Plan

If you are going to evaluate care against the treatment goals, it follows that you must write goals and objectives in clear, objective, and measurable terms. We use the word *goal* to indicate the desired outcomes of treatment. As such, goals are global and are not time limited. Treatment *objectives* are steps to the overarching goals of treatment. As such, the objectives are immediate and observable steps connected to the intervention, whereas the actual goal of treatment may be achieved long after a patient leaves the SATP. For example, the goal of reducing risk of HIV infection may be accomplished in part through a patient's treatment objective of improving his or her score on a quiz given after the patient completes an HIV education program. Your staff will need considerable training and practice in writing adequate incremental objectives if you want your program's patient records to meet criteria used by Joint Commission surveyors.

In formulating goals of treatment, your team needs to ask, "What is the outcome toward which treatment is working?" Presumably, the patient will be ready to move on to a new stage of treatment once he or she has accomplished the designated steps. For example, let us return to John Coe, who has just been readmitted to the SATP for detoxification and is scheduled to go through the rehabilitation program for the second time. Although staff referred Mr. Coe to the aftercare program at the time of his last discharge, he failed to follow through despite appointment reminders and phone calls. This patient now has expanded his stated reasons for drinking. He reports intolerable stress all around him. He has been working as a machinist and has been making errors on complicated and expensive jobs. When he goes home, there are frequent arguments with his wife about unpaid bills. His wife now refuses to answer the telephone because of frequent calls from bill collectors. The first problem might be listed as "persistent alcohol dependence as demonstrated by multiple hospital admissions and failure to follow through with outpatient treatment." A goal on the treatment plan for the rehabilitation unit would be related to the problem and perhaps stated as follows: "to avoid high-risk situations known to precipitate his relapse and to maintain aftercare treatment."

With the goal stated, the team is ready to define treatment objectives and measures for determining if the objectives are met. Staff must write these definitions carefully to avoid oversimplified statements that fail to express the complexity of the objective. Consider the following example of a poorly worded objective and measure for John Coe:

Objective: John will stop frequenting bars.

Measure: John will agree to stop frequenting bars.

This objective and its measure do not contain several important pieces of information. The formulation fails to convey information about what treatment or education the staff members plan to provide for the patient. It also fails to outline the specific steps that the patient must take to accomplish the objective. To reach this end, the treatment plan should delineate several related objectives, each specifying smaller steps to achieving the goal of sobriety.

Other missing pieces from this ill-formulated example are how often treatment is occurring and which staff members are responsible for the various aspects of treatment. Finally, the measure fails to state the immediate results expected from an intervention.

Objectives are written on three levels (Weedman, 1992). They may address whether the patient

1. Recognizes a specific fact, such as precipitants to substance abuse or certain patterns
2. Understands the consequences of the substance abuse
3. Applies appropriate principles or generalizations to correct the problem

As staff write a multilevel objective for a patient, they also devise measures to gauge how well the patient is meeting the objective. These measures for assessing the patient's progress should reflect information beyond the patient's simple agreement with the treatment objective. To measure the degree to which the objectives are met, your team needs to state objectives in terms that are compatible with observing and measuring some behavioral or cognitive change in patients. When you try to decide whether the objectives are "measurable," consider the following questions. What information will you use to assess whether the objectives have been achieved? Is this source of information readily available, measurable, and objective (as opposed to someone's opinion)? In answering these questions, you quickly see that nonobservable events should not be used as indicators of attaining objectives. Well-chosen objectives, then, do not include phrases such as *improved self-esteem* or *better*

communication. Instead, an objective related to self-esteem improvements might be "Patient reports more self-confidence in securing employment." An objective related to improved communication might be
"Patient and spouse report having two communication sessions weekly
to discuss problems." Thus you should state the measurement of the
objective in terms of specific behaviors of the patient or family members
who are the targets of the treatment.

Let us return to John Coe's treatment plan to see an acceptable
example of how the objectives and measures can better be delineated:

Objective 1:   John will recognize that high-stress days on his job should
not be followed with a stop at the local bar after work.

Measure A: During the phase of group therapy in which patients
are expected to talk about the immediate antecedents to their substance abuse, John will identify stops at the bar as a factor in his
relapses. Hour-long group sessions will be provided three times
weekly by Jennifer Monet, PsyD.

Measure B: John will recall in group therapy how difficult it was to
get in to work on time after a night of drinking.

Objective 2:   John will understand that his stopping at the bar for a
drink led to more stress at work.

Measure A: John will describe spontaneously in group sessions how
his job performance deteriorated in days following a bout of drinking.

Measure B: John will compute lost earnings from days not worked
because of drinking and will relate this lost income to his life stress
over bills in weekly meetings with Sheila Oxford, LICSW.

Objective 3:   John will develop a plan to enhance the likelihood of his
maintaining sobriety.

Measure A: In weekly hour-long sessions with his therapist, Paul
Apple, PhD, John will produce a list of stress-reducing alternatives
incompatible with stopping at a bar.

Measure B: While still in the rehabilitation program, John will
follow through with an intake interview for the aftercare clinic with
Nancy Ryan, RNC.

Progress Note on Comprehensive Treatment Planning

Progress notes entered into the patient's chart are essential to documenting both the nature and the effect of services offered to patients. It follows that your staff members should write a special progress note at the critical point when they are developing the guide to the patient's treatment. Therefore, at the same time that the team develops the comprehensive treatment plan, a team member should write a progress note capturing the flavor of the team's discussion that led to the formulation of the patient's treatment plan. This note should cover several content areas. First, the note should detail the patient's role in the treatment-planning process as well as the patient's agreement with and motivation for the plan. Second, the note should address the patient-related issues that are being deferred for subsequent treatment by explaining why a problem is deferred, what the plan for eventual remediation of the problem is, and the patient's understanding of both the reasons for deferral and the ultimate intervention plan. Third, if there has been some worthwhile discussion in the team about different approaches to the patient's treatment, that divergence of opinion should appear in the note, along with the pros and cons for each of the proposed approaches. Finally, if the type of discussion just introduced did take place, the note should terminate with information about what led the team to choose a particular method of intervention as opposed to another method. Such a note not only makes good clinical sense but also allows a record reviewer to understand the rationale for what is being done for the patient as well as the reasons for problem deferral. The following is given as an example:

John has met with the treatment team today to finalize his comprehensive treatment plan. He has agreed that he can benefit from the proposed group therapy and states that he is willing to try family therapy but is not convinced that his wife and children will come in for sessions. In addition to the stress at home, the patient has identified job-related tension as contributing to his substance abuse. He further states that this tension is at least partially caused by deficits in reading skills owing to poor educational preparation. In that the remediation of his reading skills is not within the expertise of this program, the reading problem will be deferred. The patient has agreed to be referred to an adult literacy program on discharge. Prior to meeting with the patient, there was discussion about his benefiting from attending AA meetings. The problem, brought up by the team social worker, is that the patient, who was raised as a Roman Catholic, is vehemently opposed to being exposed to interventions with a religious overtone. The concern was that the patient would confuse the spirituality dimension of AA with religion and would abort treatment. On discussion with the patient, it appeared that these concerns are warranted. Although the patient has been informed about the positive value of AA, he is unwilling to accept that program as part of his treatment and wants to find other mechanisms to support his move to sobriety after hospitalization. In weighing the possible risk of the patient's leaving treatment if staff further encourage him to explore AA versus the residual value of his receiving treatment on the unit without the AA component, the team has decided that part of the program is better than none. Therefore AA involvement will not be raised with him again during this admission. Instead, information will be provided for the patient on Rational Recovery as a possible addition to his treatment.

Special Considerations

The Joint Commission includes three special issues you need to consider under the rubric of treatment planning. First, you must consider *advance directives for medical care.* The organization must have a policy regarding advance directives for medical care if the patient develops a terminal illness or has intractable pain. The SATP's written policies and procedures should require staff members to ask about advance directives the patient may already have enacted. Staff members also should ask whether the patient wishes to make an advanced directive if he or she has not already done so. Second, you should consider the *oral health care needs* of patients if you run an inpatient or residential SATP. Written policies and procedures need to identify a minimum length of stay for which an oral health program will be carried out. Such a program includes providing emergency dental care and providing or referring patients for regular dental care. You also need to promote daily oral hygiene procedures, including proper labeling and storage of patients' oral hygiene supplies. Third, if you run a program for adolescents or children, your SATP must have a policy to promote access to *educational services for each child or adolescent served* when treatment requires a significant absence from school.

Table 4.2 displays the main areas we have addressed regarding treatment planning. It also outlines major sources of evaluation that the

Table 4.2 Standards for Treatment Planning in Care of Patients and Evidence of Compliance (TX.1 to TX.1.14)

Standards	Evidence of Compliance
Begin treatment planning process (TX.1 to TX.1.4)	Clinical records Policies and procedures manual Admissions policies and procedures Departmental manual, policies, and procedures Interviews with patients and staff
Treatment plan reflects individual's needs, strengths, and limitations (TX.1.5 to TX.1.5.4)	Clinical records Policies and procedures manual Discharge plan
Goals and objectives for the treatment plan (TX.1.6 to TX.1.7)	Clinical records
Treatment plan specifies settings, services, or programs (TX.1.8 to TX.1.9)	Clinical records Policies and procedures manual Contractual agreements Program schedule
Evaluate care against goals and make plan revisions (TX.1.10 to TX.1.11)	Clinical records Policies and procedures manual
Special considerations (TX.1.12 to TX.1.14)	Policies and procedures manual Clinical records

Joint Commission surveyor may examine to decide the extent of your SATP's compliance with these standards.

Medication Use (TX.3 to TX.3.4.1)

Medications can be an important part of treatment for SATP patients. Medications can relieve withdrawal symptoms during detoxification, treat comorbid medical and psychiatric problems, and aid in recovery (e.g., disulfiram for alcoholics and naltrexone for alcoholics and heroin addicts). The Joint Commission requires that each SATP have a functioning mechanism designed to ensure the safe use of medication (TX.3). The mechanism addresses the following:

1. The availability and prescription or ordering of medications (TX.3.1)
2. The preparation and dispensing of medications (TX.3.2)

3. The administration of medications (TX.3.3)
4. The ongoing monitoring of the medication's effect on the individual (TX.3.4)

For the most part, standards under this heading are the responsibility of the person in charge of the SATP's pharmacy or medication dispensing. We suggest that you consider asking your pharmacist to be present when the treatment teams meet with surveyors to answer questions about medication practices. The prescribing physician and the registered nurse also need to be at this meeting. One requirement under medication use that does fall to your team is that they document in the record their observations and the patient's reported perceptions of medication effects.

Nutrition (TX.4 to TX.4.6)

Most of the standards under this heading are addressed by the person in charge of your dietetics or food services. You can direct surveyors there or to the quality assurance department for relevant documents. In some settings, a dietitian may be part of an SATP treatment team. In these cases, the dietitian should be part of the group to which the Joint Commission surveyor directs questions so that the dietitian can provide direct answers related to nutrition.

You do have the responsibility to ensure that there is an assessment of patients' nutritional needs, either by a member of your team or by consult. You also need to show that your team knows how to get services for nutritionally compromised patients. If a patient needs a special diet, the patient's record should document ongoing monitoring of his or her progress.

Rehabilitation Care and Services (TX.5 to TX.5.5.6)

Rehabilitative care and services may cover a range of activities and involve treatment provided by several specialists. As stated earlier in this chapter, your staff members determine specific patient needs by studying the findings of assessments summarized on a diagnostic summary form. With the involvement of the patient (and, when appropriate, family members), staff will select rehabilitative interventions congruent with the patient's assessed needs and wishes.

At the least, the formulated rehabilitation goals will cover those living, learning, and work activities relevant to the patient. For most patients, the rehabilitation focus may take a more generalized form and involve, for example, teaching of better use of leisure time by recreation therapists, sharpening of job-related skills by occupational or vocational therapists, improvement of cognitive functioning by neuropsychologists or promotion of psychosocial skills by a therapist trained in that area. In some cases, the rehabilitative focus will need to go beyond the resources immediately at hand and may include, for example, referral to audiologists, speech pathologists, kinesiotherapists, physical therapists, or other professionals who generally are not part of your staff.

You can show that your program meets these standards by having evidence in patients' charts, in posted schedules, and in relevant policies. You also may have data from your CQM activities that are pertinent to the delivery of rehabilitation. Finally, surveyors may interview your staff and patients for more information about whether rehabilitation needs are met. The suggestions offered earlier in this chapter for treatment-planning activities are equally appropriate for formulating rehabilitation objectives and methods.

Special Treatment Procedures (TX.6 TO TX.6.6.5)

Certain treatment interventions require special clinical justification and guidelines because they pose a potential risk to the patient. The Joint Commission requires that in each SATP, the use of designated special treatment procedures have clinical justification (TX.6). If the SATP makes use of these procedures, it must have mechanisms designed to govern

1. Use of seclusion or restraint (TX.6.1)
2. Use of electroconvulsive therapy and other forms of convulsive therapy (TX.6.2)
3. Use of unusual medications and investigational and experimental drugs (TX.6.3)
4. Prescribing and administering drugs for maintenance use that have abuse potential (usually considered to be Schedule II drugs), that are known to

involve a substantial risk, or that are associated with significant, undesirable side effects (TX.6.4)

5. Use of behavior management procedures that involve painful stimuli for controlling maladaptive or problem behavior (TX.6.5)

Most of these procedures will not apply to most SATPs. The use of disulfiram (Antabuse) might be considered under TX.6.4 in that drinking while taking this medication can involve a substantial risk. Another area covered by this set of standards concerns SATPs in legal or correctional settings (TX.6.6). In such settings, the SATP must have explicit mechanisms to coordinate legal or correctional decisions with clinical decisions.

Summary

This chapter has described how to meet Joint Commission standards focused on the treatment planning and service delivery that follow the assessment of the patient's needs. Patient assessment, treatment planning, treatment delivery, and discharge are interrelated activities that at times occur simultaneously and at other times in sequence. As an example of simultaneous activities, your assessment and treatment activities are tightly interwoven, with assessment continuing throughout treatment to evaluate the effects of interventions and to provide more extensive exploration of potential problems noted on the initial assessment. We have emphasized treatment planning that includes writing individualized problem statements for the comprehensive treatment plan; writing goals and objectives for the plan; evaluating care against the objectives; and revising the plan on the basis of reassessment. If you take a sequential view of the assessment, planning, and service delivery process, you can think of treatment plan development for SATP patients as a natural outgrowth of the assessment and diagnostic phases of the treatment cycle, as a natural precursor to a patient's treatment, and as a natural lead-in to future steps in the intervention cycle.

Note

1. The standards also discuss anesthesia care (TX.2 to TX.2.4.1.1), but we will not consider these because they do not apply to most SATPs.

CHAPTER

Education

Elizabeth D. Brown
Stephen A. Maisto
Karen Boies-Hickman

The Joint Commission places considerable importance on the education of patients, their families, and others important to the patients' social environment. Its standards concern both education about improving health outcomes, and academic education. The Joint Commission's stated goals for educational components are to increase understanding of the health status, treatment options, and potential consequences of exercising options; to encourage participation in decisions about treatment; to increase the family's helpfulness in the follow-through of the treatment; to maximize the patient's skills needed in the rehabilitative and maintenance stages of treatment; to increase the patient's and family's coping

Table 5.1 Key Points in Standards on Patient Education

PF.1, .2, and .4	*Group Education* Design of curriculum content and use of needs assessment Assigning of time and resources for implementing curriculum Matching of education content to patient characteristics
	Individual Education Other educational needs tailored to individuals
PF.3	*Academic Education*

abilities as they relate to substance abuse; to enhance the patient's and family's role in continuing care; and to promote a healthy lifestyle.

Your staff members have a number of steps to take in designing and delivering an educational program. Standards PF.1 and PF.2 broadly concern such individual and family education responsibilities. This chapter discusses responsibilities for educating groups of patients as well as individual patients because of the frequency of the group format in inpatient or outpatient SATPs. The final section of the chapter briefly addresses academic education. Table 5.1 lists the chapter's key points.

Individual and Family Education Responsibilities (PF.1 and PF.2)

Education for Groups of Patients

You should first do a multipartite needs assessment for education that involves (a) interviewing patients and their families, (b) surveying other SATPs to learn the contents of their educational programs, (c) drawing on past experiences, and/or (d) consulting professional publications. Topics that may be useful include the course of substance abuse; effects on family members; effects on physical and emotional health; cognitive effects; polysubstance abuse and its effects; drug interactions; effects of drinking while taking Antabuse or "anticraving" medication such as naltrexone; effects of drinking while taking psychotropic medication (e.g., antidepressants, anxiolytics, neuroleptics); community resources such as Alcoholics Anonymous (AA), Al-Anon, and Alateen, as well as other non-AA-related self-help groups such as Rational Recovery and

Save Our Sobriety; and how to improve nutrition. If you use community resources as part of your education program, you can help patients by providing pamphlets or similar media describing those resources to patients in your setting.

Once staff members have identified the desired information content, they should explore the resources available for delivering it. In this stage you assign specific educational responsibilities to specific interdisciplinary SATP staff (as indicated in standard PF.4), you designate time slots for delivering the material, and you write policies and procedures documents describing the effort. We strongly recommend that you undertake a CQM approach when you initiate new sessions/training groups to ensure that you are meeting the educational intent. If you find a significant number of patients with family education needs, you may decide that a group educational approach may be more time- and cost-efficient than meeting with multiple individual family members. You might develop family groups within the treatment program proper, or you might find extraprogram support groups where you can refer patients' families.

You can use posted announcements of when educational classes take place, written syllabi of the class content, minutes from staff meetings, and CQM data to show that you have met the standard. The clinical record also should reflect the existence of the educational program for patients and their families. As such, when a staff member leads an educational session, as opposed to a psychotherapeutic one, the staff member should label the progress note as "education." In conducting and documenting education sessions, it is useful to ask patients/families to report back their understanding of educational material to show that the course information was communicated successfully. Furthermore, the act of reporting back information and its significance may strengthen the learning of it.

As discussed in Chapter 3, there should be evidence that you have exposed patients and families to didactic material that matches their level of learning. This statement means that each patient's cognitive capacity, cultural and religious beliefs, emotional state, and language must be compatible with the style and type of educational material to be presented. That is, patient education presentations must be *individualized*. Of course, similar compatibility must be determined for family education. Along these lines, programs may find it valuable to develop and administer brief "quizzes" (without creating a "test-taking" atmosphere) to help determine the level to which patients and family members processed and are able to recall the educational materials to which they were exposed. If patients or family members consistently perform poorly on the tests, assuming that the latter are valued for the educational content in question, it may be an indication that the language (written or oral) in which the educational material is presented is not well matched to its intended audience.

Relatedly, patients often have so much difficulty in reading that their ability to benefit from printed educational presentations in print is greatly reduced. If your program serves such patients, there are excellent sources available to staff for preparation of educational materials. One of these sources is a book on teaching patients with low literacy skills by Doak, Doak, and Root (1985). In addition, the National Institutes of Health have published a guide on developing effective print materials for low-literate readers.

Education for Individuals

Other educational needs may become apparent for the individual patient. For instance, some patients may need referral for job training or for preparation for taking a General Equivalency Diploma (GED) examination. In other cases, patients may be able to take advantage of higher education. When patients are veterans of the military services, they may be able to use earned benefits from the Department of Veterans Affairs to assist in paying college costs.

Opportunities abound for individualized education. For example, the medical history and physical examination provide a perfect opportunity not only to gather information from the patient but also to conduct patient education. Although it is best not to use such information confrontively as a "scare tactic," the objective evidence provided in the history and physical examination may help the patient to recognize both the damage done as a result of the substance abuse and the risks of continuing such abuse. As a case in point, although some patients may be aware of the potential for alcohol abuse to damage the liver, they may be surprised to find that it has also contributed to the development of problems as mundane as hemorrhoids. The use of visual aids, pamphlets,

Table 5.2 Evidence That Surveyors Might Use in Evaluation of the
Degree to Which Programs Comply With Education Standards

Written announcements of education classes
Written class syllabi
Minutes from clinical team staff meetings
Policies and procedures manual
Clinical records (mainly progress notes)
CQM data
Administrative documents

or brief summaries should be considered for patients to take with them subsequent to the physical examination.

Academic Education (PF.3)

Joint Commission standards also cover academic education. In this regard, programs should identify and provide educational resources that patients need to meet the program's educational objectives. A specific part of these standards concerns the academic education of children and adolescents, which may be provided directly by the programs or by arrangement with individuals or organizations outside of the program. The major sources of evidence of meeting the academic education standards are the policies and procedures manual, administrative documents such as program budgets, and reports to relevant committees or to the program's governing body.

Summary

A program of education is a vital part of your SATP's intervention package. Some education is best delivered to groups of patients or families; other educational efforts may be targeted at the individual. Regardless of the level at which the material is presented, it must always be congruent with the learning abilities of individual patients and each member of their individual families. Table 5.2 lists sources that surveyors might use as evidence of the degree to which programs meet education standards.

Because the achievement of a program's education goals may involve the delivery of a number of components, you may find it useful to keep for each patient a checklist of the program's educational components and the date when the patient or his or her family members were exposed to the components. Appendix D of this book presents a sample of items and a format for such a checklist, which could become part of the patient's medical record.

PART 2

Organizational Functions

Improving Organizational Performance

Timothy J. O'Farrell
Elizabeth D. Brown
Stephen F. Gibson
Norlee K. Manley
Margot G. Savage
Karen Boies-Hickman

Several approaches exist to help your SATP improve organizational performance. The CQM approach encompasses a philosophy of management and subsumes well-known practices of quality assurance methods, utilization review processes, and risk management activities. The management philosophy integral to CQM involves operating a program in which both service providers and management decide program direction, rather than having top management dictate program decisions. Although the Joint Commission does not require that you use a CQM process, surveyors will expect that your staff members have gathered and used objective information in evaluating both programs and provision of services. Moreover, the Joint Commission does use several key CQM concepts in its standards. We recommend that you adopt the CQM perspective because most health care organizations find it useful and efficient and it is consistent with the Joint Commission standards.

Methods of assessment, treatment, and treatment planning, and the process by which staff record them, may vary from program to program, and the specific criteria set forth by the Joint Commission may change from year to year. Yet an underlying steady element is needed in deciding how to assess, treat, and discharge patients. If you provide a thorough, respectful, and timely process, conducted and recorded in a way consistent with your own written policies and procedures, that process is likely to be adequate for Joint Commission purposes.

This chapter begins with an overview of the process of improving organizational performance. This initial section covers how you can develop evaluation mechanisms and instruments, how you can collect and interpret the evaluation data, and how you can carry out specific program improvements based on the findings of your data collection. The next two sections provide extensive examples of the performance improvement process (a) for key dimensions of SATP performance and (b) for important SATP functions set forth in the *MHM* (Joint Commission, 1995). The final section examines new developments in the Joint Commission's requirements for the performance improvement process contained in the revised standards. Table 6.1 lists the key points in the Joint Commission standards about improving organizational performance.

The Process of Improving Organizational Performance: Data for Program Decisions and Changes

Your decision making and planning for action flow from gathering and carefully analyzing objective data so that you can recommend changes and take appropriate action. CQM activities are complex in that you need to consider the whole system of care and how any changes that you recommend might affect other parts of the treatment system. Yet the data gathering itself can be simple and straightforward. Table 6.2 describes the steps you take in gathering and evaluating CQM data for

Table 6.1   Key Points for Improving Organizational Performance

Plan (Pl.1 to Pl.1.1)	Appropriate disciplines collaboratively plan and carry out a systematic organization-wide approach to designing, measuring, assessing, and improving SATP performance.
Design (Pl.2 to Pl.2.1.4)	New processes are designed well and are based on • SATP mission vision and plans (Pl.2.1.1) • Needs and expectations of patients, staff, and others (Pl.2.1.2) • Up-to-date information (e.g., practice guidelines or parameters) (Pl.2.1.3) • Performance and outcomes in other SATPs (e.g., reference databases) (Pl.2.1.4)
Measure (Pl.3 to Pl.3.5.2.2)	The SATP systematically collects data about • Measures of both processes and outcomes (Pl.3.1) both for priority issues chosen for improvement and for continuing measurement (Pl.3.2) • Views of patients, staff, and others about relevant dimensions of performance (Pl.3.3 to Pl.3.3.2) • Performance in all the functions identified in the *MHM* (Pl.3.4) • Processes that affect a large percentage of patients, place patients at serious risk if not performed well, or are problem prone (Pl.3.4.1 to Pl.3.4.1.3) • The SATP's use of medications (Pl.3.4.2.1) • The appropriateness of admissions and continued treatment (Pl.3.4.2.2) • Risk management and quality control activities in clinical laboratory services and nutrition services (Pl.3.5 to Pl.3.5.2.2)
Assess (Pl.4 to Pl.4.2.2)	Assessment of collected performance improvement data includes • Using statistical quality control techniques to compare data about the SATP's processes and outcomes internally over time and in relation to external programs (reference databases), standards (practice guidelines or parameters), and best practices (Pl.4 to Pl.4.1.2.3) Intensive assessment of undesirable variations in performance that include • Important single events, patterns, or trends that significantly and undesirably vary from those expected (Pl.4.1.3 to Pl.4.1.3.1)

(continued)

Table 6.1 Continued

| | • Performance that significantly and undesirably varies from that of other organizations or from recognized standards (PI.4.1.3.2 to PI.4.1.3.3)
• Already good performance that the SATP wishes to improve (PI.4.1.3.4)
• All significant adverse drug reactions (PI.4.1.3.5)

When assessment findings concern an individual staff member's performance:
• This is shared with the individual, and clinical leaders determine its use in peer review and periodic evaluations of licensed independent practitioners' competence and privileges (PI.4.2 to PI.4.2.1).
• Clinical leaders determine the competence of individuals who are not licensed independent practitioners (PI.4.2.2). |
| Improve (PI.5 to PI.5.3.3.1) | SATP decisions to make improvement or to correct undesirable performance consider
• Opportunities to improve the functions described in the *MHM* (PI.5.1.1.1)
• The factors listed above under "Measure" (PI.5.1.1.2)
• The resources needed to make the improvement (PI.5.1.1.3)
• SATP mission and priorities (PI.5.1.1.4)

The design or improvement activities
• Consider the expected impact on the relevant dimensions of performance (PI.5.2.1)
• Set performance expectations for the improved processes (PI.5.2.2)
• Measure the performance (PI.5.2.3)
• Involve those staff closest to the design or improvement activity (PI.5.2.4)

The design or improvement activities focus primarily on what needs improvement and include
• Planning the action (PI.5.3.1)
• Measuring and assessing the action's effect (PI.5.3.2)
• Implementing effective actions (PI.5.3.3) |

program decisions and changes. We now move to a more detailed discussion of these steps and how they fit into the Joint Commission areas for improving organizational performance: Plan, Design, Measure, Assess, and Improve.

Table 6.2   Steps Involved in Gathering and Evaluating CQM Data for Program Decisions and Changes Organized Under Joint Commission Areas for Improving Organizational Performance

Plan (Pl.1 to Pl.1.1) and Design (Pl.2 to Pl.2.1.4)	Decide what will be measured and how.
Measure (Pl.3 to Pl.3.5.2.2)	Measure the indicator(s) selected in Step 1.
Assess (Pl.4 to Pl.4.2.2)	Organize findings in an easily interpretable manner. Interpret findings. If they indicate a need for change, marshall resources to effect that change.
Improve (Pl.5 to Pl.5.3.3.1)	Make the planned change, and measure the changed product. Decide whether the planned improvement has occurred. If it has, then conclude that the new procedures are better than the old, and proceed to the next project. If the planned improvement has not occurred, try various solutions until the needed improvement occurs. During the entire process, document each step.

The Planning and Design Process (PI.1 to PI.2.1.4):
Deciding What to Measure

In a CQM program, staff members gather data both for program improvement and for continuing measurement. You will want data addressing the Joint Commission's dimensions of care ("doing the right thing" and "doing the right thing well"). In getting data, you will need to consider both patients' and staff's needs and expectations. You also will want to know how well these needs and expectations have previously been met. Other useful information might involve learning about your staff's perceptions of their program and ways to improve it. We suggest that you next look at your program's structure, process, and outcomes. You need to measure the performance of specific processes in all the individual-focused and organization-focused functions covered in this book and in the *MHM* (PI.1.3.4). Later in this chapter, we consider examples of CQM activities related to assessment, treatment planning, and other key functions examined by the Joint Commission.

You can select the specific indicators on several bases (PI.1.3.4.1 to PI.3.4.3):

1. Those that affect a large percentage of patients
2. Those that place patients at serious risk if not performed well, if performed when not indicated, or if not performed when indicated
3. Those that have been or are likely to be problem prone

Try to select indicators that will help you improve important aspects of your program. For example, if your program lacks the capacity to provide aftercare following detoxification, that lack will affect many of your patients. If staff members fail to assess a patient's potential suicidality, he or she will be at heightened risk. Your indicators should include some process indicators. Consider these examples: Do your patients understand a segment of a critical educational component? Is a patient's admission warranted from a utilization review perspective? Are your patients sufficiently educated about the effects of drinking while on Antabuse? Other indicators include those related to outcome: Is your patient able to maintain sobriety in the community for a given number of days? Finally, indicators include those that are likely to be problem prone. As a case in point, if you know that assessments often have failed to detect the presence of PTSD and that aftercare has been problematic because of the untreated symptomatology, an indicator for PTSD detection may be warranted.

There are no hard and fast rules saying that any one particular indicator must be used. You need to develop or select indicators based on your own program's needs. Although the Joint Commission does not mandate any specific indicators to measure, it does specify areas that you must measure. Beyond those already discussed, these areas include

1. Processes related to the organization's use of medications, including prescribing or ordering medication, preparing and dispensing, administration, and monitoring the medications' effects on patients (PI.3.4.2 to PI.3.4.2.1)
2. Processes related to determining the appropriateness of admissions and continued treatment (utilization management activities) (PI.3.4.2.2)
3. Risk management activities and quality control activities in clinical laboratory services and nutrition services (PI.3.5 to PI.3.5.2.2)

Besides the examples of indicators provided in the present chapter, you may want to read those in *Patient Records in Addiction Treatment*

(Weedman, 1992). As you go on, you will need to strike a critical balance in deciding how extensive your data-gathering activities should be. If you define the program of study too narrowly, you may overlook some critical factors, but an overly inclusive CQM program may require so much staff time that it interferes with direct patient care. Moreover, frustrated and unhappy clinicians have been known to sabotage large-scale CQM evaluation projects that do not have personnel hired specifically for data gathering and data management. We recommend a thorough and reasonable approach in evaluation. For most programs, this approach means a CQM plan that your staff can accomplish within their assigned duties.

Measurements to Improve Organizational
Performance (PI.3 to PI.3.5.2.2)

Measuring Key Indicators

Measurement of key indicators involves a written procedure for observing and recording treatment and other events. The intent is that two average persons, following only the written procedures and observing the same event, assign the same value to it or describe it in the same way. You cannot measure everything all of the time, so you often will rely on strategies such as sampling. Sampling involves observing a few instances of a phenomenon and inferring from those few instances the condition of all. Most of us are aware of sampling patients. We randomly check 10 records or so out of 100, and if all of them are in good shape, we check no further, assuming that all records are about the same.

Measurement can be as simple or as complex as you want it to be. For example, you can use a simple outcome measure by counting the number of patients who need readmission for detoxification within a certain period after having completed a rehabilitation program. Or you can use a complex method to develop questionnaire instruments as process or outcome measures. Such a complex method might involve sophisticated item-response scaling to decide scoring options, psychometric theory to create the items themselves, or scientific study to determine the reliability and validity of the measure. If you choose to pursue a more complex approach, you may want to ensure that one of your staff members is knowledgeable in instrument construction or that expert consultation is available from some source outside the team itself.

Generally, we advocate that most programs use simple, cost-efficient indicators that current staff can develop and use. More complex methods and measures can be carried out after the team has used simpler indicators successfully.

Refining and Retiring Indicators

CQM involves a continuous process of improving program activities; you refine existing indicators to make them more useful and retire indicators that no longer yield new information critical to maintaining program quality. You refine an indicator to clarify it or to stimulate further program improvements. An example of clarifying an indicator comes from an SATP that had adopted the indicator of "rectal exams documented on physical assessment" as an indicator of adequacy of physical assessment. To meet the standard, at least 90% of patients' charts had to show evidence of such an examination. Initial chart reviews frequently found "exam deferred" or "patient refused exam." CQM reviews scored these entries as "exam not performed," indicating that staff did not meet this standard. Consultation with the medical service provided guidelines related to patient age and medical history for when it was medically appropriate to defer this examination. Once the CQM committee clarified the indicator in light of these guidelines, the team decided that the standard was met.

An example of refining an indicator to stimulate further program improvements comes from an SATP that had adopted the indicator "assessments are complete" to measure adequacy of assessment. To meet the standard, at least 90% of patients' charts had to contain a complete biopsychosocial assessment. Initially, the CQM reviewer considered the assessment complete if clinicians had written something in each section of the assessment form. After a few quarters, patient charts consistently met or exceeded this standard. Then the team refined the indicator so that a complete assessment required that clinicians write the specific information required by each section of the assessment form. Thus a higher level of performance was required to meet the standard. Refining the requirements for meeting standards for important indicators can be a useful method for gradually improving program functioning. It also can provide a way for you to reinforce small changes in staff behavior.

For this to work, you need to include your staff in the CQM process and to tell them that the standard will become more difficult over time so that they do not become resentful.

You retire an indicator when it no longer serves its intended purpose: That is, it no longer leads to improvements in the program. The most common reason for retiring an indicator is that performance on the indicator consistently equals or exceeds the standard set for the indicator. For example, an SATP had adopted the indicator "progress notes document patient involvement" in formulating the patient's comprehensive treatment plan as one of the effectiveness of treatment indicators. To meet the standard, at least 90% of patients' charts had to show such evidence. Monitoring this indicator for three quarters showed that patient charts throughout the SATP consistently exceeded the standard. On the basis of this high level of compliance, the team decided to retire this indicator. The team also decided to conduct yearly reassessments with this indicator to find out if the high compliance continued. After retiring the indicator, the team chose a replacement indicator of treatment effectiveness.

Assessing Data (PI.4 to PI.4.2.2) and
Making Improvements (PI.5 to PI.5.3.3.1)

Organizing Findings

We recommend that you display CQM data in an organized fashion so that they are accessible and easy to understand. You need to consider the specific method that will be most useful to display the program's CQM data. Besides using a sometimes instructive but usually less compelling style of typed data, you may want to consider a data presentation with more visual impact. For example, "storyboards," which display results graphically in an attractive manner on poster boards, can say more in a glance than a table replete with numbers. Figures 6.1 and 6.2 presented later in this chapter are examples of graphical display of CQM data.

We also recommend that you keep CQM information in one place, such as in a loose-leaf book. Develop an indicator directory and place it as the first piece of information in the book to serve as a table of contents. List indicators that you are actively monitoring first, followed by pending indicators and then by retired indicators. For each entry, note the name of the staff member responsible for providing data about the indicator. The directory also provides information about the threshold for taking action on an indicator and the time period during which indicator data are gathered. This table of contents gives a quick overview of the program evaluation material that is available from your CQM activities. You can use another loose-leaf book to file minutes from your program meetings and any of its subordinate functions (e.g., CQM minutes, credentialing minutes).

The above suggestions represent the basic elements of data management. In some cases, you may want or need a more sophisticated approach. For example, if you have computer capacity, you may decide to use a database program to organize and display CQM findings. In any case, you should assemble a thoughtful, organized indicator book to enhance the meaningfulness of the indicators for your surveyor.

Turning CQM Findings Into
Systematic Program Improvement

At times, as an SATP is evolving, CQM findings are positive, both affirming and facilitating movement in new programmatic directions. At other times, data from a CQM indicator or information about a solitary event may suggest that a program is failing to meet preordained standards and that, as a result, treatment may be substandard. In any of these cases, interventions and changes that are initiated must be followed by intensified assessment to determine the nature of the impact from the altered program. If, during these assessments, you have questions about the performance of a privileged individual staff member, the Joint Commission requires that you inform the medical staff of the problem. Ultimately, the medical staff decides whether the information will be used in the process for reprivileging. Should the problem individual staff member not be privileged as an independent provider, the relevant department head, if applicable, must be informed about the process.

When deciding to make improvements on the program, you must be mindful of the functions designated as important by the Joint Commission, you must know what resources you have to make the improvements, and you must assess the fit of the proposed changes with both your program's and your parent organization's (if you are part of one) mission and priorities. We recommend that you involve staff who will be affected by any program changes as you

1. Consider the effect anticipated from the change
2. Specify performance expectations related to the change
3. Adopt, adapt, or create measures to be used in assessing the effects of the change

You should place greater emphasis on correcting processes that need improvement than on developing new program components that will not take the place of those in need of improvement.

We have been impressed with two key aspects that have led to improvements through the CQM process. First, feedback to staff of information about indicators of SATP functioning can be very powerful. The feedback focuses your staff on key areas for improvement and allows them to see positive change that occurs over time. Quarterly or more frequent CQM reports to all of your staff can provide this feedback. You also can send these reports to relevant department heads and to hospital management to keep them informed of progress and to enlist their assistance when needed in the CQM process. Second, through this process, you can increase communication and coordinate problem-solving efforts among units and staff within your program. This development may be the most important mechanism for change. In the specific CQM examples cited in this chapter, solution of the problems revealed by CQM indicators required extensive dialogue and cooperation among SATP staff members.

Using CQM Minutes to Document the
Performance Improvement Process

We suggest that you use minutes of the SATP's CQM committee to document each step in the CQM process described above and listed in Table 6.2. Concise minutes should document the initial indicators and rationale for their choice, the results of measuring the indicators, and action steps taken to deal with results observed. Most important, you can show in the minutes the process of program improvement through detection of inadequate program functioning and corrective action. Thus your minutes should show an ongoing process in which you refine or retire indicators as the standards are met, so that your team moves on to new aspects of program functioning that need improvement. You may find the following format useful for recording minutes. First, give the *topic*. Next, present the objective *findings*. Third, present the *conclusion*. Fourth, list *recommendations*. Fifth, describe the *action* to be undertaken and the agent responsible for that action. Finally, specify an expected completion date and a *follow-up* date when the committee will consider the topic again. Although at first this format may seem contrived and confusing, with experience and practice it evolves into an easily managed method for concise and thorough recording.

Examples of the Performance Improvement Process for Key Dimensions of Performance

In the latest revised standards, the Joint Commission details definitions of dimensions of performance. The dimensions include "doing the right thing," a category that addresses the efficacy and appropriateness of an intervention in the context of the patients' needs, and "doing the right thing well," a category that includes the availability, timeliness, effectiveness, and continuity of assessments and interventions. This category also covers patient safety, the efficiency with which you provide services, and the respect and care you give to the patients.

Doing the Right Thing

Efficacy

In determining the efficacy of treatment, you make judgments about patient outcome. The question of interest here, then, is the degree of improvement gained by your patients. When you develop an indicator, you also establish a threshold. This threshold for action serves as a red flag to initiate action. As an example of assessing efficacy, an SATP has developed the following outcome indicator related to effectiveness of treatment and has specified its threshold:

Indicator: Patients who relapse or discontinue aftercare treatment in the first month following inpatient rehabilitation treatment

Threshold: More than 45% of discharged patients

In this example SATP staff recently found that the established threshold was being exceeded. During the previous 3 months, 50% of the patients had resumed their substance abuse within a month of discharge. The team needed to understand why this increase had occurred. The cause for the increased rate of recidivism was not immediately evident. Therefore, the team did an in-depth analysis to detect common factors among the relapsing patients that might account for their poor outcomes.

If you did this type of analysis, you might go in two directions. First, you could examine those treatment components with which most of the recidivists were treated. For example, if most of the recidivists were treated in group therapy, you would want to know if the group was being held in the form and intensity needed. Second, you could examine whether patients who had certain things in common were not treated with a component that was needed. For example, if many of these patients were married and had not received marital or family therapy, you might decide to intensify your referrals for that treatment modality. This type of analysis might point to needed changes in what your program had to offer. For example, if many recidivist patients were from a specific ethnic group, you would need to decide if clinical staff representative of that group needed to be added or if present staff needed education to work better with the ethnic group.

After analyzing possible causes for the indicator threshold being exceeded, you decide which program changes to make to correct the problem. You also continue to measure the indicator to find out whether it falls below threshold after you make program changes. You may have to repeat this procedure a few times before you discover solutions to the problem. For example, the team at an SATP might decide to add more intensive work on relapse prevention to their treatment program. This addition might reduce relapses in the first month after discharge from the rehabilitation program, but continued monitoring might show that dropout from aftercare treatment still exceeded the threshold. This further information might prompt the team to make additional program changes to emphasize more strongly the importance of aftercare. Monitoring would continue and this time might show success in bringing both relapse and aftercare dropout below threshold.

Appropriateness

Under the heading of "Appropriateness," the Joint Commission requires that any test, treatment, or discharge plan be appropriate to patients' needs. For example, one inpatient alcoholism program used an assertiveness questionnaire as part of a screening battery because assertiveness training was a growing focus of the program. After a period of review, staff discovered that none of the patients scored in the normal range on the questionnaire and that the data derived were not helpful. As another example, you must be concerned both about false-negative and false-positive scores from a cognitive screening procedure. In the first case, you would have faulty data that would lessen the chance of treatment success; in the second case, there might be a tendency to generate unnecessary referrals to a neuropsychologist, thus wasting resources.

Doing the Right Thing Well

Availability

Under this heading the Joint Commission addresses whether you make assessments, procedures, treatments, or services available to a patient who needs them. We suggest that clinical disciplines providing care to your patients develop a memorandum describing in detail what is offered, who provides what is offered, and with what frequency it is offered. A dietetics department might address nutritional counseling. A recreation department might describe its program of activities. Social work might specify its role in assessment or care delivery. When some clearly identified need exists that your program cannot provide, you should find a way to make it available. Many SATPs may not have a neuropsychologist on staff, but your cognitive screening may show that some patients need a neuropsychological assessment. You can arrange through contracting or referral to have necessary neuropsychological testing done. At one SATP shortly before a Joint Commission survey, the only vocational psychologist qualified to do vocational assessments was on an unplanned and extensive sick leave. Contracting with an agency in the community allowed the SATP to show that it could provide vocational assessments when needed.

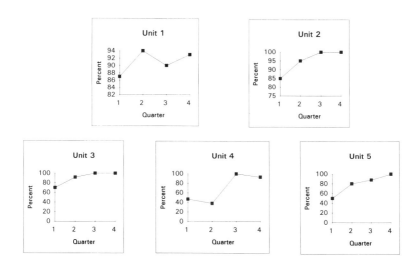

Figure 6.1. CQM Monitor for Effectiveness of Treatment in Five Units of a Large SATP (90% = Threshold)

Timeliness

Timeliness of work completion must be considered throughout the cycle of substance abuse treatment. As said earlier, the Joint Commission mandates that a complete medical history and physical examination be done and documented for each patient within 24 hours of admission to an inpatient SATP. Another timeliness requirement, discussed in Chapter 10, demands that records be complete within 30 days after a patient's discharge.

Effectiveness

Interest in effectiveness focuses on whether care is given in the correct way to achieve the desired outcome. The indicator labeled "comprehensive treatment plan addresses clinical problems noted in the biopsychosocial assessment" provides an example. The standard was that at least 90% of patients' charts on each of the five units making up the SATP needed to show such evidence. Figure 6.1 presents the CQM monitoring data over time for this indicator. Monitoring showed that patient charts in the three inpatient units (#1-#3) of the SATP consistently met or exceeded the standard after the first quarter. Performance was worse in the outpatient units (#4 and #5) at the start and took more quarters of monitoring and investigating the problem before it met the desired standard.

The CQM coordinator discussed the disparity across units with the unit coordinators and the CQM committee. Eventually it became clear that inpatient staff members were identifying certain problems at the end of the assessment and deciding to defer the treatment of these problems until the patient was discharged to outpatient treatment. Such problems included chronic medical problems presenting no acute distress but requiring outpatient follow-up and serious family problems that the inpatient team legitimately decided to defer for later attention. Thus these problems did not have to be listed on the inpatient comprehensive treatment plan because they were not being treated there. However, the outpatient units were expected to review the inpatient assessment and address these problems that had been deferred until the outpatient phase of treatment. When the outpatient teams failed to include these deferred problems in the outpatient comprehensive treatment plan, the outpatient teams failed to meet the standard.

Identification and solution of this problem led to several improvements in the functioning of the SATP. At first, outpatient clinicians often did not review the inpatient assessment because they did not realize that they were supposed to do so. Educating the staff about the importance of continuity of care and the philosophy of an integrated continuum of care helped. In addition, often the inpatient assessment and medical records were not available for outpatient clinicians because the discharge summary had not been dictated or transcribed. These shortcomings led to efforts to solve this problem. Solving the problem also created a dialogue between inpatient and outpatient teams that clarified which problems should be deferred to outpatient care and which should not. Communication while solving the problem also clarified the role of each team. By year's end, all units met the standard. They continued to do so for the next 6 months, at which time this indicator was retired. Thus using the CQM process produced the desired compliance with the indicator and, more important, improved the functioning of the SATP by changing the processes underlying the indicator.

Continuity

We suggest you consider continuity of care not only through the various phases of the continuum within the SATP but also with aftercare in the community. Program documents, such as policy memoranda, patient flowcharts, organizational charts, and functional charts help demonstrate the SATP's continuum to surveyors. Your patient records should provide immediate evidence of a viable continuum of care within your overall program, which may range from detoxification to rehabilitation to aftercare. You should have available contracts with community agencies and a record of patient placement at these agencies as good supporting evidence to show surveyors. To be maximally effective, this record should be accompanied by data showing the success of each patient in following through with the community agency. Problems should be recorded when they occur, and the corrective actions should appear on data sheets and be reflected both in minutes for SATP staff and in CQM reporting. Finally, when SATP staff members refer patients for aftercare, they should forward patient information to help the aftercare agency ensure continuity of care.

Safety

The Joint Commission requires that SATPs maintain a safe environment for patients, staff, and anyone in the SATP setting. Safety concerns include the simple acts of making sure that corridors and doors are unblocked and afford free access. They also include truly dangerous situations, such as those involving weapons or physical fighting or fire. Again, we advocate written material to guide staff and to demonstrate your policies to the Joint Commission. Any safety memoranda written by whatever body handles safety at your facility should be available in your SATP program manual. Emergency procedures (such as sounding alarms) and telephone numbers should be displayed prominently. Staff should have extensive safety training during orientation and have refresher training on an annual basis. They should be well versed in resuscitation methods and evacuation strategies in case of fire. You should document this staff training in attendance logs or in other appropriate sources. At one SATP, fire procedures and emergency codes for the alarm system are printed on the back of staff identification badges. "RACE"

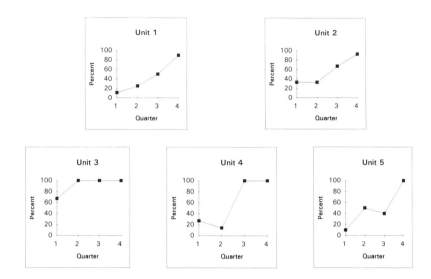

Figure 6.2. CQM Monitor for Adequacy of Assessment in Five Units of a Large
SATP (90% = Threshold)

(Rescue, Alert, Control, Extinguish) directs immediate action, and
"PASS" (Pull, Aim, Squeeze, Sweep) activates a fire extinguisher. Emergency phone numbers for police and fire also are printed on the backs
of identification badges that are to be worn during duty hours.

Efficiency

Efficiency of care considers the relationship between patients'
outcomes and the resources used to deliver care. An example deals with
the adequacy of assessment. A standard labeled "sexual orientation is
documented on the biopsychosocial assessment" required that at least
90% of patients' charts show evidence of this documentation. The intent
of this indicator was to discover whether patients had any special
treatment needs related to sexual orientation. Monitoring showed uni-
formly low compliance at the start across all five units of the SATP. Only
Unit 3, in which the SATP CQM coordinator worked as a staff person,
improved on this indicator quickly. The remaining units gradually improved over time, but it took nearly a year before they exceeded the
indicator threshold. Figure 6.2 presents this CQM monitor over time.

The CQM coordinator and staff of each unit and the SATP's CQM committee discussed the problem with this indicator at length. This dialogue revealed several reasons that performance on this indicator was deficient and resistant to change. Most SATP staff members were not comfortable discussing sexual orientation or sexual issues with patients. Some staff had philosophical resistance to asking questions about sexual orientation. Others felt it was intrusive and violated patients' rights. Still others attacked the requirement as yet another example of "political correctness" by the liberal government bureaucracy that they objected to on ideological grounds.

Eventually, the CQM committee took two approaches to solving this problem. The first approach was to address it during a refresher course conducted for staff on Joint Commission standards. This course addressed problem areas related to program compliance with Joint Commission standards identified through CQM monitoring or other methods. The CQM coordinator discussed the problems with the assessment of sexual orientation matter-of-factly along with other SATP problem areas. He emphasized the intent of the Joint Commission standards related to this indicator. The Joint Commission requires an assessment for individualized treatment planning that takes into account any special treatment needs a patient might have related to sexual orientation (or other factors, such as ethnicity or age). In addition, the CQM coordinator gave specific suggestions on how to ask questions about sexuality in a way that would be comfortable for most patients and staff. Staff members who were already comfortable with such questioning reported how they did it, and this information seemed to help considerably.

The second approach was for the CQM coordinator to discuss the issue with the staff of each unit during monthly CQM chart reviews. Again, he treated this indicator as one of several areas needing improvement and listened respectfully to staff concerns and objections. He repeated the rationale for this indicator, using the same low-key, matter-of-fact style that had characterized the refresher course. He was careful not to get involved in a heated debate about the issue. As you can see in Figure 6.2, by the final quarter of the first year for this indicator, all units in the SATP were in full compliance. The CQM committee decided to continue monitoring this indicator for a second year to be sure that compliance continued.

Respect and Caring

Surveyors assess the degree to which staff members include patients in care decisions. Your medical records should show patient involvement both in the content of progress notes and in the patient's signature on treatment plans. You can show additional evidence of patient involvement with a team calendar showing times when patients met with the treatment team.

Under the heading of "Respect and Caring," surveyors also assess the sensitivity of your staff members as they interact with patients of varying ethnicities, abilities, needs, and expectations. Evidence of such sensitivity might come from orientation materials, from interviews with patients, from satisfaction ratings, from observations on how the staff interact with patients, and from a log designating accounts of staff counseling to improve sensitivity.

Continuous Quality Improvement and SATP
Policies and Procedures

The various policy and procedure documents discussed in this chapter are part of your program's structure. It is important that you remember that all policies and procedures and other documents in the manual must themselves be included in the CQM approach to program management. You need to stay updated on the documents that guide the program and to make changes in either the documents or the program when a lack of congruence is found.

Examples of the Performance Improvement Process for Important Functions in the MHM

The Joint Commission requires that you compile CQM data for each of the important SATP functions that is the subject of a chapter in the MHM. We include next examples for some major functions, including assessment, treatment planning, patient care and education, and the continuum of care. You may first want to examine Table 6.3, which lists areas that may be of interest to surveyors.

Table 6.3 Surveyor Sources of Information for Improving Organizational
Performance (PI.1 to PI.5.3.3.1)

Committee reports and minutes

Discussions with leaders and quality improvement staff and teams

Training materials

Planning and design documents

Design specifications

Performance criteria for new processes

Plans for data collection

Review of measurement strategies and plans, data displays, measurement and
improvement reports

Review of data on needs and expectations of patients, staff, and others

Strategic, quality, and other planning documents

Plans for review and documentation of ongoing reviews

Improvement strategies and plans

Assessment conclusions and reports

NOTE: These sources of surveyor evaluation material apply to all or nearly all the performance improvement standards.

CQM in Assessment

CQM for assessment activities involves determining in which ways assessments are incomplete, inaccurate, or unnecessary. The most important CQM questions, from a vulnerability assessment viewpoint, concern those related to lethality assessment. You will need to show morbidity and mortality review procedures for patients who complete a suicide during or after treatment and a review procedure for those patients who become violent or attempt suicide post treatment.

Other important areas of assessment also merit your review. For patients who are active in aftercare, follow-up contacts with the aftercare agencies can be optimal times to receive feedback about the accuracy of the assessments. You can monitor the percentage of patients who reach aftercare with major problems unaddressed. In the worst case, you might discover how many patients reached aftercare with assessments not completed. In other cases, the feedback could address the accuracy of the assessments. For example, some aftercare agencies have noted problems in which PTSD symptomatology secondary to sexual abuse was not identified. Others have reported that patients demonstrate greater cognitive impairment than reported on the inpatient assessment. Some aftercare programs have reported that the assessment of substance abuse was incomplete for drugs other than the major substance of abuse noted. Acquiring data on topics such as these provides additional CQM information on continuity of care.

CQM in Treatment Planning

There are several ways to think about continuous quality improvement in the context of the treatment planning activities. Chapter 4 of *Patient Records in Addiction Treatment* (Weedman, 1992) presents some of these: Treatment plan reinforces AA involvement; ongoing clinical problems, when they occur, are addressed in treatment plan; and continuing care plan addresses unresolved problems as noted on the problem list. It would take little to develop other useful monitors: Are all problems identified in the assessment of the patient either covered in the treatment plan or deferred in a note? Is there a note explaining the reason for deferring some identified need for treatment? Are objectives appropriately delineated?

What may be even more useful is study of the need to revise treatment plans. You may recall that we earlier raised the possibility that such revisions could be related to patient variables, to treatment variables, or to errors in either the assessments used in treatment plans or the reasoning by which a particular treatment or set of interventions was chosen. Careful study, then, of reasons for plan revisions can be helpful to your program and the patients it treats. If it turns out that a significant number of revisions are caused by changes in patient-related variables, you need to determine whether you need to broaden the program's assessment process to consider a wider range of information. If you find a number of revisions related to unplanned program changes, you may want to take action to correct the problem. If revisions reflect errors in the assessment/treatment selection processes, you may decide that staff need education or clinical supervision. Alternatively, you may learn that new assessment procedures should be incorporated or that new treatment options need to be made available. If you determine that the need for revision is related either to errors in assessment or to poor decisions in matching treatments with patients, you have the information to take steps to remedy the problem.

CQM in Patient Care and Education

One of the more interesting questions to answer in assessing patient care and education is whether the intervention or educational input that the patient was supposed to receive did in fact occur and, if it did, whether it occurred in the manner designated. In his classic paper "The Three Faces of Evaluation: What Can Be Expected to Work," Quay (1977) introduced this process variable and showed that outcome evaluations are often worthless in that the lack of treatment precludes anything other than spontaneous improvement. Thus it behooves you to develop mechanisms for ensuring that treatment or education does get delivered. Moreover, if an element is not being delivered, you should note its absence in some type of log so that any subsequent follow-up data can be evaluated in the context of the missing service. We suggest assessing the integrity of the educational components either by quizzing patients and their families or by interviewing them about what they learned.

CQM in the Continuum of Care

CQM activities also may be useful for evaluating your organization's continuum of care. For example, periodic analyses of referrals to and within the SATP are quite valuable from a utilization review perspective. If you find that your program receives many referrals of patients who do not meet the admission criteria, you have a clear signal either that there needs to be more educational emphasis on what constitutes an appropriate referral or that the criteria need more precise delineation. From another direction, study of the referral practices may reveal that an indiscriminate referral practice is leading patients to be sent to several aftercare clinics. This problem is particularly likely to occur when eligibility standards are being strictly applied and the likelihood of a negative decision for program entry is heightened. For example, if aftercare services are being restricted to patients with extensive insurance coverage, there may be more difficulty in developing an aftercare option. Being aware of the strong possibility of a patient's not being admitted to any one aftercare program, clinicians may be tempted to take a "shotgun" approach by sending aftercare referral forms to several programs, rather than taking the more traditional approach of waiting for any one program to evaluate and refuse entry and following this rejection by referral to another program. From a time expediency viewpoint, the "shotgun" practice makes sense. Nevertheless, if patients are left with multiple incompatible clinical aftercare assignments, their treatment will surely be disjointed, a negative outcome from both utilization review and quality assurance perspectives. If you find such a practice, you will have evidence that the policy and procedure memoranda describing the referral process need to become more specific. Problems with transfers from one program component to another in multisite SATPs (e.g., detoxification or residential care in one location and aftercare in another) are a potentially troublesome area. A problem of this magnitude needs ongoing monitoring on a case-by-case basis to resolve disruptions in care and to incorporate new practices into existing procedural documents.

New Developments in the Joint Commission's Requirements for the Performance Improvement Process

The revised Joint Commission standards for improving organizational performance contain several new developments, some of which will present substantial challenges to many SATPs. The following quote from the *MHM* addresses this point:

> Finally, the scoring guidelines for this chapter have been designed to help organizations envision the long-term goals of the standards and make progress toward those goals. The activities described in this chapter will take varying periods of time to implement fully, requiring various types and levels of change, and may require resource acquisition or reallocation. Thus, expectation for full compliance with many of these standards will be phased into the survey and scoring process at a pace consistent with the field's readiness.[1]

These comments suggest that SATPs need to take these new requirements seriously and show considerable progress toward meeting the new standards. They also suggest that Joint Commission interpretation of the standards will become stricter as time goes on. Therefore, we shall consider some of these new developments briefly.

Collaborative, Interdisciplinary Approach

The new standards require a collaborative, interdisciplinary approach to systematic, organization-wide efforts to improve performance (PI.1 to PI.1.1). It is no longer sufficient to have improvement activities carried out within parts of an SATP (e.g., within outpatient services or within inpatient services) or within professional disciplines (e.g., among nurses or among social workers). Some CQM indicators may be localized to specific units or disciplines if they represent unique issues for those areas, but it will not suffice if the majority of improvement activities are of this type. The Joint Commission (1995) specifically addresses this point in describing the intent of standards PI.1 to PI.1.1:

> Although the units or subgroups can be considered involved, it is clearly not in a collaborative manner. Until improvement activities become collaborative (across services, between clinical and administrative staff, and, when appropriate, interdisciplinary), they will be difficult for an organization to plan and provide for a systematic and organizationwide approach.[2]

The earlier examples in Figures 6.1 and 6.2 about effectiveness of treatment and adequacy of assessment in five units of a large SATP followed the recommended approach. An SATP CQM committee with representatives from all units in the SATP designed the indicators. The CQM coordinator collated the results of the indicators and presented them to the CQM committee. Once they were approved by the CQM committee, a quarterly report presented the monitoring results to all SATP staff, to discipline department heads, and to the director's office of the hospital in which the SATP was located.

Measure Both Process and Outcome

Another new requirement is that the SATP systematically collect data about measures of both processes and outcomes (PI.3.1) and use the results to plan program improvements. The increased emphasis on outcome measurement is new. The Joint Commission (1995) described the intent of this standard:

> A "balanced" measurement and assessment system includes measures of both processes and outcomes—outcomes to understand the results, processes to understand what has been done to cause those results. For example, the outcomes of many processes are not evident or measurable at discharge, or they vary considerably due to patient variables. It is prudent to measure the processes that most profoundly influence outcome.[3]

Many SATPs have considerable uncertainty about what "outcome evaluation" they should do. We suggest that programs start by identifying key intermediate patient outcomes. These midway treatment results are necessary precursors to ultimate desired outcomes (e.g., substantially reduced substance use and improved life functioning 1 year after treatment as compared with 1 year before treatment). The following are sample intermediate patient outcomes:

1. Completing agreed-upon treatment
2. Maintaining abstinence during the first, second, and third months after starting treatment
3. Attending at least two AA meetings a week during the first, second, and third months after starting treatment
4. Attending at least 90% of scheduled aftercare meetings a week during the first, second, and third months after starting treatment
5. Doing one or more of Indicators 1 through 4

Most SATPs have the resources and expertise to measure and assess these intermediate outcomes. Such a CQM project is likely to come up with changes that the SATP can make to improve these intermediate outcomes.

Ideally, we wish all SATPs would conduct state-of-the-art evaluations of the longer term outcomes of their patients. However, most programs are not ready to undertake such study, and doing a poor job can waste resources and produce criticism from a knowledgeable surveyor. "Let's send a questionnaire to all our patients 6 months after they complete inpatient or partial hospital treatment to see how many still are abstinent." This suggestion, or something very similar, frequently arises when SATPs consider outcome evaluation. A year later, after considerable work, 20% of the intended patients have returned questionnaires, many of which are incomplete. Staff question the validity of some responses because information from other sources contradicts the reports of sobriety by some of the patients. At this point SATP staff and leaders have little to show for their efforts at outcome evaluation.

If you decide to conduct a long-term outcome evaluation study, we urge you to consider the following suggestions. First, plan it carefully. Get an expert consultant to help you design your evaluation plan if your staff does not have this expertise. Consider the cost carefully in staff time for collecting and analyzing the data and preparing reports. Get the needed information from patients to locate them over the course of the follow-up study. Second, do a high-quality study of a smaller sample rather than a poor-quality study of a larger sample. Generally, you will need to sample from your patient population rather than to try to follow up all your patients. If your program treats 600 patients a year, a sample of 15% to 20% is good. Third, use accepted measures to collect enough data from each patient to reach valid conclusions about your patients' outcomes. Consider using the Timeline Follow-Back (TLFB; O'Farrell & Langenbucher, 1988; Sobell & Sobell, 1996) interview for information on substance use, the Addiction Severity Index (McLellan et al., 1985) to measure problems in multiple life areas, and the Reasons for Relapse Interview (Maisto, McKay, & O'Farrell, 1995) to describe relapse triggers. To get accurate information, conduct interviews in person with the patient and a collateral informant; also, give alcohol breath tests at each interview and drug urine screens as often as you can afford. Fourth, consider this schedule of data collection. Begin with baseline data collection near the start of treatment. Conduct the first follow-up 4 to 6 weeks after baseline and the remaining follow-ups at 3, 6, 9, and 12 months after baseline. Fifth, return to your consultant or staff expert for help in analyzing the data and preparing a report. Such an outcome evaluation study will teach you a great deal. If executed properly, it will withstand scrutiny. Finally, if your SATP cannot do such a long-term follow-up study, stick with evaluations of intermediate outcomes as described above.

Examine SATP Performance Internally Over
Time and in Relation to External Standards

Another new requirement is that assessment of collected performance improvement data should compare data about the SATP's process
and outcome measures of performance both (a) internally over time and
(b) in relation to external programs (reference databases), standards
(practice guidelines or parameters), and best practices (PI.4 to
PI.4.1.2.3). Most of the CQM examples given in this chapter have
concerned processes measured and evaluated internally over time. For
example, Figure 6.2 showed improvement over time in the adequacy of
information about sexual orientation in the biopsychosocial assessment
for five units in a large SATP. This type of data represents a process
variable measured internally over time. The one outcome indicator
example we discussed, concerning the percentage of patients who relapse
or stop aftercare treatment in the first month following inpatient rehabilitation treatment, represents an outcome variable measured internally
over time. These are the types of CQM indicators with which most of us
are familiar.

The new standards require you to compare the performance of your
SATP with external sources of information. The intent is that your SATP
not only should show improvement over time but also should move
closer to external markers of performance. The Joint Commission (1995)
described this further:

Information from external sources should be as up to date as possible,
such as recent scientific, clinical, and management literature; well-
formulated practice guidelines or parameters; reference databases; and
standards that benefit from periodic review and revision. . . . To move
organizations toward this goal, the compliance expectations will be
increased incrementally over the next few years. . . . Most organizations
are currently able, or will be in a short period of time, to obtain and use
information from such sources as the literature and practice guidelines
or parameters. The initial expectations will thus be high.

Fewer organizations currently participate in external reference
databases or will in a short period of time be able to do so. The initial
expectations for such sources will thus be modest. These reference databases to which the standards refer are those designed to accept data from
the organization and provide feedback on the organization's per-

formance compared to other organizations and in a form useful to the organization (for example, adjusted for differences in patient population). In 1995, organizations will be expected to contribute to one such external database in assessing their performance. Examples of such databases are those operated by multi-site systems and national provider organizations.[4]

A few examples may help. Research shows that one third to one half of patients treated in public-sector inpatient alcoholism treatment programs relapse within 90 days of discharge (Institute of Medicine, 1990). On the basis of this information, an SATP in a VA medical center set a CQM standard that the relapse rate in the first 90 days after inpatient discharge would not exceed 45% of patients. On the basis of practice guidelines, another SATP decided to comply with standard PI.3.4.2.2 by using the American Society of Addiction Medicine patient placement criteria to evaluate the appropriateness of admissions to different levels of care within the SATP. Finally, another SATP in a VA center contributed data to a national VA database that included information on staffing patterns, average length of stay, patient volume, recidivism, and so forth. This SATP was able to convince its medical center management that it should add two staff members because its patient volume was substantially greater than the national average but its staffing level was lower than the national average. The added staff allowed a program reorganization to provide additional services that the CQM committee had determined were needed.

Summary

In this chapter we have provided a guide for the process of continuous quality improvement. CQM involves a change from a top-down leadership approach dominated by upper management to an empowerment of clinical teams and middle managers who are accountable for the functioning of the SATP. We have examined the steps involved in gathering and evaluating CQM data for program decisions and changes. We also have included examples of CQM at work in a large, complex SATP. Finally, we have described key mechanisms for improvement through the CQM process, regular feedback about program functioning, and increased communication and coordination among SATP units and staff.

Notes

1. © *The 1995 Accreditation Manual for Mental Health, Chemical Dependency, and Mental Retardation/Developmental Disabilities Services (MHM).* Oakbrook Terrace, IL: Joint Commission on Accreditation of Healthcare Organizations, 1995, Vol. 2, p. 229. Reprinted with permission.

2. © *The 1995 Accreditation Manual for Mental Health, Chemical Dependency, and Mental Retardation/Developmental Disabilities Services (MHM).* Oakbrook Terrace, IL: Joint Commission on Accreditation of Healthcare Organizations, 1995, Vol. 2, p. 229. Reprinted with permission.

3. © *The 1995 Accreditation Manual for Mental Health, Chemical Dependency, and Mental Retardation/Developmental Disabilities Services (MHM).* Oakbrook Terrace, IL: Joint Commission on Accreditation of Healthcare Organizations, 1995, Vol. 2, p. 237. Reprinted with permission.

4. © *The 1995 Accreditation Manual for Mental Health, Chemical Dependency, and Mental Retardation/Developmental Disabilities Services (MHM).* Oakbrook Terrace, IL: Joint Commission on Accreditation of Healthcare Organizations, 1995, Vol. 2, p. 249. Reprinted with permission.

CHAPTER 7

Leadership

Elizabeth D. Brown
Norlee K. Manley
David B. Mather
Karen Boies-Hickman

Good leadership is essential to the development and maintenance of your program. As described in the *MHM* (Joint Commission, 1995), the goals of leadership are to plan, direct, implement, coordinate, and improve services. You, as a leader, have the responsibility for providing direction and definition. Further, you and your staff need to follow up on these responsibilities by communicating well with patients, their families, the community, and the treatment facility proper. We say more about leadership in Chapter 12.

Organizational Planning

In the course of meeting *MHM* criteria for program planning, you will face certain definitional tasks in preparing program memoranda. You will need to answer:

1. What is your program's mission?
2. Which elements make up your program?
3. How does your program operate?
4. How do you operate a continuous quality improvement effort that monitors and modifies itself and your service providers?
5. What is your strategic plan?
6. How does that plan fit with the mission of the program and any parent treatment facility?
7. What means of communication do you have for staff members?
8. How do you communicate with patients, families, the community, and other parts of your treatment facility?

As you answer these questions, you can develop policy and procedure memoranda, which themselves are a nucleus from which your program manual can emerge. The manual details all aspects of your treatment program. These aspects include your mission, your goals and objectives, your scope of care and guidelines for operation, your criteria for admission, your criteria for type and timeliness of patient assessments and treatment planning, your method and record of staff credentialing, your ongoing staff education, your contractual arrangements, your methods of referral, and your CQM plan. We also recommend that you include any parent facility's bylaws and other written materials related to the SATP and your patients.

We suggest that you request copies of program descriptions, policies and procedures memoranda, position descriptions, mission statements, and vision statements from fellow program managers. You can adapt these materials to fit the specific needs of your own program.

Mission, Vision, Values, and Strategic Planning

As a starting point for your program, we recommend that you develop a mission statement, a vision statement, and strategic, operational, and programmatic plans for the program. You develop these plans and documents by evaluating the treatment needs of patients who are the responsibility of your treatment facility. These patients may live in a given geographic catchment area, or they may be patients for whom you have contractual responsibilities.

For example, four affiliated medical centers exist within a 50-mile radius. Although three of the four medical centers have detoxification services, only one has a rehabilitation program. Thus that center's mission statement might acknowledge a wider responsibility for rehabilitation treatment and a narrower one for detoxification. The Joint Commission also expects a connection between your mission; your strategic, long-range, and operational plans; your budget and resource allocation; and your policies. For example, one program has the following mission statement: "The mission of the SATP is to provide a rehabilitation program for the treatment of patients with problems resulting from substance abuse." After an assessment that many patients discharged from the detoxification ward were relapsing and not receiving rehabilitation services, the program leaders proposed that they transfer patients directly from detoxification to an intensified outpatient rehabilitation program. To accomplish the program that the leaders planned, they needed to strengthen staffing, an accomplishment that required reducing inpatient rehabilitation beds. Because the leaders were familiar with the facility's funding mechanisms, they convinced management that reducing inpatient beds made sense both from a perspective of improving patient care and from a cost savings view. The program leaders could use the paper trail behind these decisions to show surveyors who might question the change.

Planning involves all aspects of care delivery covered in the first five chapters of this book. We recommend that you address each of these functions and develop policy and procedure memoranda that specify the steps your staff will follow in providing adequate and timely care. To produce these documents, you must know patients' and staff's perceived and actual needs, their expectations, and practice guidelines. For this last element, you may rely on experience gained in other settings, a consultant, or a review of the professional literature.

In planning the timing of assessment or care activities, you must consider the environment in which services are to take place. For example, it may be unrealistic to assume that an outpatient substance abuse program in which appointments are each separated by a week's time should have a bank of assessment data comparable to what can be obtained within 2 to 3 days in an inpatient setting. Besides having policies and procedures about the timing of care activities, you may want to develop clinical pathways. Pathways can help keep your staff aware of where patients should be in their cycle of treatment. For example, an inpatient rehabilitation pathway might call for a completed physical workup in 24 hours; completion of other assessments by the end of Day 3; introduction of education, treatment, and discharge planning on Day 4; and discharge by Day 14. Although some may view our advocacy for clinical pathways as getting away from individualized treatment, that is clearly not our intent. In fact, the individual patient going through the course of care is receiving treatment components selected on the basis of his or her needs. Moreover, we know that some patients progress faster than the average patient whose experiences are reflected in the development of the pathway and that others may need longer to gain sufficient benefit from treatment. The Joint Commission does not specify particular pathways or time frames; rather, it expects programs to set such standards themselves and then to demonstrate adherence. Further, surveyors will expect that you have attended to factors resulting in deviations from standards.

Systems theory stresses that what happens in one level of an organization has an impact on other levels. Therefore, you need communication channels to involve upper-level management in decisions with policy ramifications. An organizational chart is useful in this process and can be illustrative to site visitors. Other means for showing relationships come from various memoranda, minutes, and bylaws. For example, at one medical center there is a clinical management team (CMT) consisting of leaders of the SATP. This group reports directly to a mental health and behavioral sciences executive group. That group, in turn, reports either to a larger mental health and behavioral sciences council (MHBSC) or to the deputy chief of staff (DCOS) for mental health, depending on the nature of the policy decision. We return to this organizational structure to demonstrate how it is used later in this chapter. Leaders have minutes from any of these governing bodies to illustrate planned action.

Patient Care Services

The Joint Commission's Standard LD.1.3 specifies that plans for providing services should be consistent both with assessed patient need and with the mission of the organization. To meet this requirement, you develop specific criteria to define who is suitable for treatment, transfer, and discharge and the means for making these decisions. In generating these criteria, you draw information both from a recognition of the patient population's needs and from the resources available for treatment. You then write up these definitions with sufficient detail so that there is no question about which patients are likely to benefit from services. For instance, admission to an SATP might use criteria such as "Patient has at least a 3-month-long history of excessive and frequent substance abuse; patient expresses need for help in stopping substance abuse." Admission to some component programs of the SATP may require additional and more specific criteria: For example, a program dealing with comorbidities of substance abuse and PTSD might require 60 days of sobriety before entry into the program. The rationale might be that the patient should be past a critical period in recovery from substance abuse before beginning work on PTSD. An SATP's inpatient detoxification unit might exercise a criterion of daily alcohol intake equivalent to a fifth of liquor for the past 10 days.

Planning Patient Assessments, Treatment Planning, and Treatment

You will need to define the sequence for individualized assessment, treatment, and treatment planning. We recommend that you meet Standard LD.1.3.4 in a way that recognizes both the need for an individualized approach and the necessity of an ongoing process of continued assessment, treatment planning, treatment monitoring, and treatment plan revision. The documents that you produce should show recognition of services both within a given phase of care and throughout the continuum of care available in your SATP system. To guide staff members in this ongoing cycle of assessment, treatment planning, and delivery, you need to ensure that policy and procedure memoranda are comprehensive and have sufficient detail. We recommend that you develop written guidance on activities such as what constitutes adequate practice in, for example, (a) individualized assessments with a biopsychosocial emphasis, (b) individualized treatment, (c) diagnostic summaries, and (d) biopsychosocially based treatment plans. To meet the requirement of sufficient detail, we recommend that you delineate specific information such as the time frames for completing activities and the designation of staff responsibility for the various aspects of assessment and treatment planning. In this document, it is important that you outline the necessity and means of referring patients for assessments and/or services unavailable within your SATP. Particularly for freestanding SATPs, memoranda specifying relationships with other treatment facilities are crucial. When contractual arrangements exist, you should state them.

In writing the memoranda describing the above care practices, you should acknowledge both similarities and dissimilarities across your various settings. For example, there may be overlap among the biopsychosocial assessment procedures in detoxification and rehabilitation. On the other hand, some methods may be quite dissimilar. For example, many SATPs have developed specialty treatment tracks for geriatric patients, gay and lesbian patients, trauma survivors, or dual-diagnosis patients. Some specialized programs may require more specific or focused assessment procedures, above a standard biopsychosocial assessment.

We advise that you include a complete description of treatment modalities to facilitate the development of an individualized set of treatment experiences for each patient. What you need here goes beyond the typical description of treatments, which themselves may fall under the categories of group therapy, individual therapy, assertiveness training, relaxation, stress management, family therapy, vocational counseling, or leisure education. In specification of an intervention, you need to say which staff members are qualified to deliver it, which types of patient problems it is designed to ameliorate, with what intensity and frequency it is offered, and what its objectives are. We also recommend that you pay careful attention to developing and describing treatment interventions for specific patient populations based on gender, age, sexual orientation, or ethnic origin. Finally, you specify the mechanisms that your staff will use in making referrals. As you plan your continuum of care, we recommend that you think about the strengths and weaknesses of the referral linkages. At one facility some linkages may be well established: For example, an eligible intoxicated patient appearing at the hospital's emergency room is admitted for detoxification if there is a bed available. Other linkages may still be at an exploratory stage: For example, how does the newly developing satellite program connect with the main-site detoxification program to get an intoxicated patient admitted as an emergency case when no transportation is available? Attention to the question of quality of transfer will allow your staff to know where to put program development efforts to enhance continuity of care. Problems of weak linkages are critical areas for resolution in your strategic planning process.

It is also important in the strategic planning process that you not overlook the functional relationships of your program with other treatment facility programs. Your staff members have to reach out from their micro-organizational structure to get patients' needs met. For example, staff members need to negotiate patient care needs with the medical service in treating a homeless substance-abusing patient who needs both detoxification and treatment for acute pneumonia. Formally writing the procedures used in accessing services outside of the SATP lessens ambiguity in the referral process and enhances the continuum of care.

Planning for Discharge

In the current era of delivering a quality level of health care as economically as possible, you will need a policy for discharge planning. This policy memorandum should fulfill multiple purposes. First, it should reinforce the need for continuity of care from inpatient to outpatient status or from one outpatient program to another. Second, it should stress that discharge planning addresses the patient's care needs and desires as determined by a reassessment at the discharge-planning stage. Third, the document should specify the need to involve patients and, when indicated, their family members in the discharge-planning process. Fourth, the policy statement should address the need for timely and direct communications with programs to which you refer your patients. Finally, the document should establish a mechanism for assessing the efficacy of the discharge-planning process. In this last regard the document provides direction on the method for determining sample size and the specific types of data you will gather. Relevant data may include determinations of the appropriateness of the referral, the adequacy of patient follow-through, patient satisfaction with the new program, and information on recidivism.

Collaboration in Designing Services

We suggest that you collaborate in planning with the staff most knowledgeable about the services. Site visitors can examine documents describing the planning process to find out whether the planning committee is sufficiently knowledgeable about the range of programming provided.

Services Are Designed to Be Responsive
to the Needs of Patients

Although the literature on the value of patient satisfaction ratings is quite mixed, there still is considerable reliance on the idea of seeking patients' and their families' opinions of services rendered. Part of the criticism about satisfaction rating research relates to the quality of instrumentation used. The Joint Commission expects to see indicators of patient satisfaction; we encourage you not to reinvent the wheel. We advise using an instrument that has undergone fine-tuned psychometric development and testing. For example, researchers at the centralized VA Patient Satisfaction Center have expended considerable care and evaluation on their instrument development and validation.

Services Are Available in a Timely Manner

Once you have developed detailed memoranda, including the timing of various services, you might also want to incorporate data on compliance with the requirements into your CQM activities. This evaluation may involve looking at logs, taking samples of charts, or relying on data produced by other facility services to which you have made referrals. From completing some recommendations listed earlier, you should be aware of the resources available for patient care. You should also know how they fit with your patient care needs.

At times, you may find patient care needs that you cannot meet within your program or your treatment facility. In such instances, your plans should show mechanisms for getting these patient care needs met by referral, contracting, or consultation. Moreover, you should show that the alternate mechanism is acceptable to your facility medical staff. One example given previously dealt with SATPs in small hospitals where there were no services for neuropsychological assessments. In such a case, you would contract only with licensed professionals who met the eligibility and credentialing criteria used for professional staff.

We advise that you have materials about referrals and contracting available, both for assistance to program staff and for examination by site surveyors. For example, a resource guide that provides referral resources and contains copies of contractual arrangements may be helpful to staff in arranging patient discharges or transfers. Moreover, in that Joint Commission surveyors request information about referrals and contracts, having the materials preassembled in one place is a strategically good practice. If the material in the resource guide is not voluminous, you might include it in the program manual.

Setting Priorities for Performance Improvement (LD.1.4)

The Joint Commission requires that you have studied priorities in your planning activities. As noted in Chapter 6, priorities include processes that affect many patients; processes that place patients at risk if not performed well, performed when not indicated, or not performed when indicated; and processes that have been or are likely to be problem prone. We suggest that you write your plans in such a manner that it is clear that the priorities were considered.

The issue of priority setting also includes a sensitivity to emerging needs identified by measurement and assessment. One way to assess whether your program is on target is to do an occasional comparison between the program goals, the goals and objectives of various treatment elements, and the goals specified for patients on their treatment plans. If a lack of congruence is found, you will know that you need to update documents so that they reflect an updated means for meeting the treatment needs of the patients. This examination should also extend to the treatment requirements for various specialized groups and to changes in the patient population, the community, regulations, or the treatment environment.

You also need to be alert to changes introduced by fluctuation in the population you serve. As an example, VA medical centers had to adjust their care to a new cadre of veterans who served in Desert Storm. This influx brought in proportionately more female veterans than had been in previous combat populations. It also brought in more young veterans with families in which a parent's health needs were interfering

with children's well-being and development. The treatment requirements for these veterans and their families required changes in planning,
mission, policies, or procedures at programs serving such patients.

In a sense, our suggestion that emerging treatment requirements
may demand changes in the direction of your program and your documents resembles a practice with which line staff members have great
familiarity. These staff members review and revise individual patients'
treatment plans either because of some new factors related to the patients
or because of patients' reactions to certain interventions. So, too, you
should periodically review and revise your program's "treatment plan."
Therefore, we suggest that you develop a system for monitoring the
documents that guide your program at least annually. This type of
monitoring can demonstrate to Joint Commission surveyors that you
engage in ongoing oversight of your mission and structure. A file can be
kept of obsolete copies of mission statements, policy and procedure
documents, and so forth, that the surveyor can compare to updated ones.
You can also show that you review and update your documents in your
program's annual or semiannual reports and in formalized program
minutes.

Annual Operating Budgets (LD.1.5)

The Joint Commission expects that you present your budgetary
requirements to management through whatever mechanism exists at
your treatment facility, with appropriate documentation. It also expects
annual auditing, a process that your fiscal department arranges and
conducts. You should refer surveyors with questions about the budget
and auditing to your fiscal staff or back to the quality assurance staff.

Uniform Performance of Patient Care Processes (LD.1.6)

The availability of carefully delineated criteria for admission to any
given level of service should help you in meeting Standard LD.1.6. You
may find it useful to show orientation materials in which you say how
screening staff should use criteria. Moreover, you can address the topic
in staff meetings and enter discussion into minutes. Surveyors may look
through medical records or may use observations of patient care activity
in determining whether you have met the standard.

Scope of Services Performed by Each Department (LD.1.7)

For Standard LD.1.7, we recommend that you show surveyors the written and approved policies and goals of the departments that provide services to you. Surveyors may scrutinize minutes, reports, memoranda, patient records, or any other pertinent material to determine if the service provided is compatible with the written procedure.

Leaders Participate in the Organization's
Decision Making (LD.1.8)

The content of this standard is fourfold:

1. Development of your patient care programs, policies, and procedures describing how patients' care needs are assessed and met
2. Development and implementation of your plan for providing patient care
3. Participation in your decision-making structures and processes
4. Implementation of an effective and continuous program to measure, assess, and improve performance

To pass the standard, you will need documentation that you have worked with representatives of other relevant departments in formulating your program's structure, plans, development, and CQM program. You may show evidence of having met the standard through minutes, cosigned documents, and memoranda showing memberships on various committees.

Recruitment, Retention, Development, and
Education of Staff (LD.1.9)

The ability to attract and keep good staff is integral to acceptable patient care. Thus the Joint Commission puts a premium on how you recruit and treat staff. To meet the standard, you should consider seven factors when developing programs for recruitment, retention, development, or staff education:

1. Your mission
2. The case mix of your patients, as well as the degree and complexity of care required by them and their significant others

3. The technology used in patient care

4. The expectations of the treatment facility medical staff, patients, and their significant others for the type and degree of patient care provided

5. The stated, felt, or otherwise identified learning needs of staff members engaged in patient care

6. Mechanisms designed for recognizing the expertise and performance of staff members engaged in care delivery

7. Those issues identified or stated by your staff members that influence their decision to continue employment with the organization

You might show surveyors written plans for staff retention and education, minutes, reports of staff education attendance, and advertisements for staff recruitment. The Joint Commission has noted that leaders should give retention of good staff priority over recruitment in the organization's planning. You should know and use principles of sound organizational management in reducing staff turnover and in promoting good morale in the workplace. The well-known tenets of making staff feel appreciated, acknowledging their good work, sharing information with them, and soliciting their opinions should come naturally to leaders familiar with the empowerment-of-line-staff theme central to CQM.

Directing Services

Surveyors will want to find that you and other leaders in your SATP are effective in your roles. Further, the site visitors will expect that you work competently with your staff to promote an acceptable level of patient care. Essentially, the surveyor will want to see that you have carried out the tasks discussed earlier in this chapter. Thus the Joint Commission associates many activities with standards under this heading. Table 7.1 addresses major areas for consideration.

The first two elements of these standards (LD.2.1.1 and LD.2.1.2) merely require that program leaders work with the rest of their organization in coordinating and integrating patient care. For a maximum score on LD.2.1.3, you need to show that you have participated in policy planning and review. You also need to show that the planning documents are readily available to program or service staff. You can meet this requirement easily by locating a three-ring binder filled with up-to-date program memoranda in a centralized space.

Table 7.1   Standards Related to Leadership's Direction of Services and
Evidence of Compliance (LD.2.1)

Standards	*Evidence of Compliance*
• Program integration into primary functions of the organization • Coordination and integration of services within program • Recommending a sufficient number of qualified and competent personnel • Determining the qualifications and competence of staff who are not independent providers • Continuous quality improvement • Maintenance of applicable quality control programs • Staff orientation, in-service training, and continuing education • Determination of and recommendations for space and other resources • Selection of and liaison with off-site services • Implementation of a defined set of patient rights and responsibilities • Establishment of a means of accountability to governing bodies and functions • Receipt of and action on committee and program reports and recommendations • Establishment and implementation of clinical policies and procedures • Specification of staff disciplines' clinical care roles • Verification of staff licensure/ certification/registration • Determination of the current competence of all clinical staff	• Patient handbooks • Staff meeting minutes • Interviews with patients and staff • Organizational and/or functional charts • Relevant reports • Position descriptions and performance evaluations of leaders • Relevant memoranda • Program/staffing changes • Program memoranda delineating approved clinical programming with references for sources of approval (e.g., professional associations, widely accepted guidelines); attachments to the memoranda delineating the roles of various clinical disciplines • Staff position descriptions • Copy of written material describing the credentialing/privileging procedures used by the SATP, by professional departments, by your professional standards board • Staff performance appraisals • Any relevant CQM data pertinent to individual clinicians' performance • Peer review data • Action plans

For LD.2.1.4 and LD.2.1.5, you need to show that you recommended an adequate number of qualified staff members and that the recommendation was based on your assessment of your treatment population's needs. We recommend that you return to your planning documents used for assessing staffing needs. From these materials, you can retrieve whatever information you gave to administration. You will also want material on the means by which you determine the qualifications and competence of patient care delivery staff members who are not licensed independent providers. For this need, you can go in one of two ways. If you are in a matrix-managed system, you will need to specify whatever review and supervision process you use. If, instead, you are in a department-managed system (e.g., nurses are administratively responsible to a nursing department), you can look to the relevant department for assistance with this task.

Surveyors do not score LD.2.1.6 under leadership but instead consider it along with the standards covered in Chapter 6 of this book. Your direct oversight in implementing *all* quality control programs required for your program is necessary for a maximum score for LD.2.1.7. Standard LD.2.1.8 deals with staff orientation and continuing education. Here you need at least two types of evidence for a maximum score. First, we recommend that you have available staff attendance records showing continuing education on grounds or in the community. These hours include education relevant to clinical work. Second, you will need to show that you have collaborated with other staff for larger scale educational requirements related to safety management, infection control, emergency preparedness, and so forth. Your role in these educational programs is to identify and address staff training needs regularly.

The next two standards, LD.2.1.9 and LD.2.1.10, concern your assessment and requests for adequate space for programming. In the first of these standards, the space requests are within the physical space of the organization. You merely have to show that you directed a memorandum or other communication through channels. For a maximum score, your record should establish that you have been consistent both in forwarding all necessary space recommendations and in forwarding them through appropriate organizational channels. The second of the standards is for off-site space. Here you need simply to show that you have assessed the need for space and made the appropriate recommendations.

Standards LD.2.1.11 through LD.2.1.17 are relatively uncomplicated. Many of the examples listed as methods for choosing compliance in Table 7.1 are applicable to these standards.

In LD.2.2 the leadership standards address the question of whether your governing body has allocated adequate staffing resources to care for your patients. Appropriate sources of information exist in various reports, minutes, budgets, and staffing patterns. This set of standards covers three basic elements. First, it concerns definition, quality, and appropriateness of your leadership. You will want to show a copy of signed-off administrative privileges that specify your program management role. The surveyor will also expect that the clinical aspects of your program are the responsibility of a clinically trained and experienced professional staff member. The surveyor does not score the standard itself (LD.2.2. 2.1.) Rather, the Joint Commission provides it to clarify the range of professional clinicians who have a background adequate for a clinical leadership role. Second, the LD.2.2 standard covers the responsibilities of multiple leaders and of team members. We recommend that you delineate the duties of your staff as program leaders or as team members. In the former case, the administrative privileges that you use for each program leader should outline each leader's scope of authority. In the latter case, you can define team members' roles on the team through a written description, staff minutes, and team member interviews.

Finally, LD.2.2 focuses on the adequacy of your staffing during the 12 months before the survey. We suggest that you have a copy of your staffing patterns, copies of contracts with other service-providing agencies, and copies of any memoranda outlining consultative services from other departments in your organization. You will also need material illustrating adequate professional nursing care, with the intensity of that care compatible with the clinical needs of your patients. Finally, through your written plan for clinical services or some other documentation, you can show the surveyor that your staff participated in the development of a clearly defined supervisory process. Furthermore, you need to show that you have had the supervisory process itself in place for at least the past year.

Integrating Services

The *MHM*'s standards under LD.3 deal with how you integrate your SATP with other services in your organization. Inherent in these standards are the expectations that you are involved in planning, that you communicate well with other parts of the organization, that you and your program managers are involved in improving services, and that you provide for follow-through on problematic issues. Table 7.2 provides more specificity on these major areas.

Table 7.2   Standards Related to Leadership's Integration of Services and
Evidence of Compliance (LD.3)

Standards	*Evidence of Compliance*
• Organization and functional relationships of service are specified (LD.3.1) • Leaders individually and jointly develop, participate in, and encourage (LD.3.2) • Communication within organization (LD.3.2.1) • Communication with organizations related through function or corporation (LD.3.2.2) • Policies and procedures are developed in collaboration with associated programs and approved by the appropriate organization's clinical and/or administrative staff (LD.3.3) • All managerial staff participate in cross-organizational activities to assess/improve organizational performance (LD.3.4) • Relevant information is sent to leaders responsible for the organization-wide performance improvement activities (LD.3.4.1) • There is a written process assigning responsibility for taking action on recommendations coming from performance improvement activities (LD.3.4.1.1)	• Organization charts • Communication memoranda, letters, documents • Contracts and/or memoranda of understanding with other organizations/ services • Organization-wide committee/executive body minutes and memberships • Interviews/discussions with staff

You ought to be able to show a surveyor how you communicate with leaders of the treatment facility. This demonstration is easiest if you can produce organizational and functional charts. We recommend that you have on hand relevant minutes from meetings attended by leaders of the various departments of your organization. For instance, in VA, each medical center has monthly clinical executive board (CEB) meetings. Minutes list the clinicians who are members of the CEB and show problems that were addressed and solutions that were engendered. Staff retreats, interdisciplinary work groups (such as found in process improvement teams), and membership on organization-wide committees (e.g., pharmaceutical or education) also illustrate compliance. You will also want to show communication strengths with other organizations with which you have a relationship (e.g., referral sources, referral providers).

LD.3 also addresses collaboration in the development of policies and procedures. We recommend that you inform staff about the process for writing and getting these materials approved. Your staff should know that you send *all* draft memoranda to relevant departments and to administration for comment before formal publication and implementation.

Finally, LD.3 focuses on your program's leaders' participation in cross-organizational activities to improve program performance. Here you may have material showing your staff on a process improvement team. Or perhaps you have staff working with another service in a performance improvement activity. For example, there may be a cooperative venture with the pharmacy service for better policing of the polypharmacy-seeking behaviors of some addicted patients. In evaluating your role in performance improvement, surveyors will look at how relevant information is forwarded to appropriate leaders responsible for organization-wide improvement. Further, the surveyor will expect that you have written materials designating the responsibility for taking action on performance improvement recommendations. A case example presented earlier best illustrates this point. One VA medical center's clinical management team (CMT) consists of a psychiatrist who is the acting director of the SATP, a psychologist who coordinates the outpatient program, a head nurse for inpatient programming, a senior social worker who supervises social work staff assigned to the SATP, and the SATP's administrative coordinator. As a decision-making group, they represent both critical services and the continuum of care. This group is in charge of the performance improvement activities in the SATP. In turn, the CMT reports to the executive group of the mental health and behavioral sciences council (MH&BSC), made up of the program leaders from psychiatry, psychology, social work, nursing, and activities. For the next line of authority, the executive group reports both to the full mental health and behavioral science committee (consisting of all mental health clinical department heads) and to the deputy chief of staff (DCOS) for mental health. If the matter is pressing, the DCOS bysteps the MH&BSC to go directly to the chief of staff, who has the power to make the final clinical decision. The matter is then introduced at the next regular meeting of the MH&BSC for informational purposes. On the other hand, if the matter does not require an immediate decision, the executive group presents it to the DCOS for informational purposes. Action is deferred until the next MH&BSC meeting. Typically, recommendations coming from this latter route next go to the clinical executive board, a group composed of all clinical department heads.

If you do not have a reporting structure that fulfills the functions just described, you may have other means that are equally effective. Your staff should be able to answer questions about whatever means you have for forwarding performance improvement information to your organization's decision makers. For example, in some settings, reports might be attached to the minutes of an overall mental health department that includes the SATP. In other settings, findings might be attached to minutes of a quality council. Or perhaps findings might be addressed in minutes from the medical staff meetings. In any case, the surveyor assesses whether your approach is congruent with the master plan of the treatment facility and whether a mechanism exists for written materials to reach the broader organization. In addition to identifying the mechanism, we suggest that your policy and procedure documents on this topic specify the frequency of reporting.

Role in Improving Performance

The survey team uses standards set out in LD.4 to evaluate whether your leaders are aware of and part of a systematic organization-wide performance improvement process. This process includes setting expectations, developing plans, and managing processes to assess, improve, and maintain the quality of the organization's performance. The dimensions of improvement include the organization's governance, management, clinical, and support activities. To get a maximum score for the standard, you not only must have the evidence just described but also must show that your leadership has participated actively in the improvement process. Table 7.3 addresses major areas covered by LD.4.

The standards go on to address the meaningfulness of your contributions to performance improvement activities. Can you show that you and your program managers have a fundamental knowledge of perform-

Table 7.3 Standards on Leadership Performance Improvement and
Evidence of Compliance (LD.4)

Standards	*Evidence of Compliance*
• Leaders set expectations, develop plans, and manage processes to assess/improve/maintain (LD.4) Quality of governance activities Quality of management activities Quality of clinical activities Quality of support activities	• Continuous quality improvement plans • CQM assessments • Documentation of interventions undertaken as a result of CQM data • Follow-up data on the efficacy of such interventions
• Leaders understand approaches and methods of performance improvement (LD.4.1).	
• Performance improvement includes Process planning (LD.4.2.1) Priority setting (LD.4.2.2) Systematic assessment (LD.4.2.3) Implementation of improvement activities/interventions (LD.4.2.4) Management of improvement (LD.4.2.5)	• Minutes from staff meetings • Chart reviews • Peer reviews • Focused problem studies/interventions • Descriptions of information and data management systems, processes, and resources
• Measurement, assessment, and improvement of important processes and activities are ongoing (LD.4.3)	• CQM training plans and records • Staff interviews
• Resources for performance improvement include adequate Assignment of personnel (LD.4.4.1) Allocation of time (LD.4.4.2) Creation or management of information systems for data collection (LD.4.4.3)	
• There is adequate training of personnel in data management processes (LD.4.4.4)	
• Leaders analyze/assess their own performance improvement contributions (LD.4.5)	

ance improvement? We recommend that you have evidence of relevant education on hand. Other useful data may come from interviews and self-report.

As surveyors begin closer scrutiny of the performance improvement activity, they judge whether your leadership has

1. Planned for the process of improvement
2. Set priorities for improvement
3. Used systematic performance assessment
4. Implemented improvement activities based on assessment
5. Maintained achieved improvements

Your leaders should be able to describe these activities and how the decision-making process went. We recommend that you convey the gist of these discussions to nonleadership staff at regular meetings. This approach will keep your entire staff informed about performance improvement, and the minutes also can capture the discussion as evidence of compliance.

The surveyor will also examine your leadership role in organization-wide performance improvement, including efforts to improve patient outcomes. We suggest that you have copies of reports that you have written or to which you have contributed that describe performance improvement studies and that convey recommendations for improvement.

LD.4.4 guides surveyors as they examine the amount of support that you give to performance improvement work. Do you have evidence showing that you have assigned enough adequately trained staff to performance improvement work? Have you given these staff members enough time to do this type of work? Which resources have you provided to assist these staff members in data management and analysis? Do they have personal computers available? If so, do they know how to use the equipment? Do assigned staff members know how to access data stored in some centralized computer bank? What is the nature of training that you have provided for your staff members to improve their ability to engage in performance improvement activities? We advise that you not only establish a paper trail answering any of these questions but also take frequent opportunities to discuss performance improvement work with your staff in both formal meetings and informal encounters.

The leadership standards end with something resembling a meta-analysis. Surveyors will examine your self-examination of how effective you have been in performance improvement activities. You must meet five criteria for showing full compliance with LD.4.5:

1. You have written material stating your performance improvement goals in objective and measurable language.
2. You have amassed data that can be used in assessing the effectiveness of your work.
3. You use predetermined methods and criteria in analyzing your effectiveness.
4. You make determinations about your effectiveness and make changes to improve your performance.
5. You engage in an ongoing process of self-reevaluation to maximize your effectiveness as a performance improvement agent.

Summary

This chapter has discussed the role of leadership in planning and implementing policies and procedures for the SATP. We have addressed the necessity for SATP leadership to take an integrative approach in program design, development, and maintenance so that the local program's management is congruent with the management of any larger organization. Finally, the chapter has focused on your leadership role in performance improvement activity. This focus has included your role in the broader organization's work, along with how well you have facilitated the involvement of your staff at both a local program level and an organizational level. We also have given attention to the need for effective communication, including a careful delineation of appropriate communication channels so that decisions important to performance improvement can be made.

CHAPTER 8

Management of the Environment of Care

Elizabeth D. Brown
Stephen A. Maisto

The topics of concern to the Joint Commission in its evaluation of the environment of care are diverse. For example, surveyors want to know how you deal with the physical environment challenges of safety, security, hazardous materials and waste, emergency preparedness, life safety, medical equipment, utility systems, and space allocation. The dimensions of interest for each of these topics include how you have designed your processes, how you have educated your staff to carry them out, how you have implemented them, how you are measuring your successes and shortcomings, and how you are correcting problems that you may have detected. In addressing these processes, you need to think about how staff should perform and to decide how you will assess staff performance in performance appraisals. Further, you will have to develop and implement procedures for identifying environmental factors of importance to your program, monitoring these factors, preventing or correcting problems, and measuring what you are doing. In addition to these environmental challenges, you need to consider the therapeutic environment, which will also fall under the scrutiny of the surveyors. Here the concerns are with whether adequate space has been allocated to your program and whether the environment affords dignity, privacy, and respect to your clients and staff. The outline used in this chapter takes you through the design, implementation/teaching, and measurement stages of meeting standards for the physical environment. The chapter ends with discussion of meeting the standards related to the therapeutic environment and the requirements for a smoke-free setting.

Design, Implementation, and Measurement (EC.1, EC.2, and EC.3)

Needs assessment and a review of regulatory requirements are the first steps in developing a plan for meeting standards relevant to the care environment. Once you have completed this initial phase, you can turn to writing the various memoranda that will both guide your program and facilitate the gathering of information to show as evidence of compliance to surveyors. The development of both the program components and the staff educational components is critical to the design stage. Other responsibilities that you will want to address are involved with developing staff performance standards related to the physical environment for licensed independent practitioners; you will need to cover the environmental requirements in the job descriptions of nonlicensed personnel. Although the other processes, teaching/implementing and measuring, are described discretely in the *MHM* (Joint Commission, 1995), they are in fact interrelated and also related to the design phase. Essentially, just as advocated in Chapter 4, there should be ongoing assessment of the environmental needs, the design of new ways of doing things to meet needs better, and ongoing education of staff as they implement program changes related to the environment of care. Table 8.1 provides a synopsis of the various activities associated with developing and maintaining an adequate care environment.

Table 8.1 Dimensions and Processes for the Physical Environment of Care

Topic	Design	Teach/Implement	Measure
Safety	Needs assessment followed by development of policy and procedure memoranda	Orientation	A staff member is appointed to collect information about deficiencies and means for correcting them
Security		Continuing education	The organization has a safety committee
Hazardous waste	Development of staff educational components	Routine operation	The safety committee analyzes environment problems and generates potential resolutions
Emergency preparedness	Development of procedures described in memoranda	Emergency procedures as needed	
Life safety		Failure detection followed by correction	The safety officer works with staff to implement recommended changes and to assess their outcome
Medical equipment	Development of staff performance standards	Staff retraining	
Utility systems	Writing of job descriptions for non-licensedindependent practitioners	Steps taken to secure adequate space for programming	
Space allocation			

133

Memoranda that you use to describe your methods of attaining a safe and secure care environment may be documents that you write specific to your setting or documents that you adopt/adapt from a parent organization. You also have latitude in how you prepare your documentation: You may choose to describe several or all elements of environmental challenges in one document, or you may choose to have multiple memoranda, each addressing just one of the environmental considerations. Once developed, these materials should be incorporated into any body of instructions given to staff during orientation. As relevant, review of the requisite parts of the memoranda should take place as part of ongoing staff education. In addition to the above suggestions, we recommend that you orient your staff to the reporting and investigating of all incidents that involve property damage, occupational illness, and client, personnel, or visitor injury. You are advised to have on hand records of staff safety education and copies of performance plans that have a safety component.

A surveyor also can be shown minutes of staff meetings in which discussions of environmental concerns have occurred. Finally, in the inpatient setting, we recommend that you introduce relevant topics into any community meetings for patients and that you have informal discussions on the subjects of safety and security with both staff and patients so that they will know what to expect if a surveyor stops to talk with them. In the case of staff, surveyors may ask not only about the *safety* risks produced in the environment but also about the mechanisms for reporting the risks and the actions that have been undertaken to correct problems.

Security is a major consideration in any substance abuse treatment environment. As you develop your security plan, you will need to consider not only the security of clients, visitors, personnel, and property but also how to provide or limit access to sensitive areas. In your documentation and in patient materials, you need to delineate the specific procedures to be undertaken by your staff when security is breached. If your program is in a larger medical center, you should keep the parent organization's plan at hand so that it is readily retrievable if surveyors ask how you would handle a given problem. As recommended in other places in this book, any plan that you develop must be congruent with your parent organization's (if relevant) master plan and must provide your staff with guidelines particular to your program. For example, you may be concerned with contraband materials being smuggled in to clients and may need to be more specific about how this problem is to be handled than the overall parent organization policy is. You may need more detail in addressing the difficulty of patients who show up under the influence of alcohol or other drugs in admitting areas or after being on pass. If you are managing an inpatient program, you may need more particulars in describing procedures to be used if patients become assaultive. You may want to have a policy stating which areas of your wards are open to patient visitors. Finally, you may want, as part of your security arrangements, a special type of door lock so that patients leaving an inpatient unit during off-peak staff hours to procure drugs cannot let themselves back onto the ward without staff notice. In addition to these security needs, surveyors will be interested in how you have provided identification for your staff, all of whom should be wearing official badges. Furthermore, you should have accessible staff education and orientation materials, staff meeting minutes demonstrating attention to security matters, and copies of performance plans that have a security element for staff. Staff should not be surprised if a surveyor engages in discussions with them to determine their range of knowledge about handling potential security problems.

You need to address handling and disposal of *hazardous materials and wastes.* If your program exists within a larger medical setting, you probably will be able to use existing hazardous materials and wastes policies for your overall parent organization in preparing for a survey. We recommend that you have on hand materials similar to those suggested in previous sections of this chapter for a surveyor's inspection. Discussions with your staff should leave a surveyor convinced of their familiarity with specified methods of hazardous waste disposal and of their knowledge about reporting requirements if something goes awry in disposing of wastes. Staff should also be conversant about the procedures to be used in case of emergency.

If your SATP is freestanding, you will need to develop policies and procedures for *emergency preparedness, life safety, medical equipment,* and *utility systems.* But if, as in many cases, your SATP is part of a larger health care organization, there seem to be few, if any, ways in which your program's treatment environments should be different from those of the

Table 8.2   Key Points Addressed in Discussion of Standards on Design and
Implementation of the Environment of Care (EC.1 and EC.2)

Create a safety management program applicable to all of the units in a program's
continuum of care.

Orient staff to reporting and investigating all incidents involving property damage,
accidents, illness, and patient, personnel, or visitor injury.

Introduce the topic of safety into patient community meetings.

Have a plan to protect the security of your program environment.

Have accessible policies on handling of hazardous materials and wastes.

Have accessible policies on emergency preparedness, life safety, and medical
equipment.

---

parent organization. Therefore, it is unlikely that you will need to develop a separate policy memorandum, and it is improbable that you will be held responsible as a program manager for ensuring that your programs are in compliance with the standards. You will be expected to be responsible for being informed about the parent organization's policies, to ensure that your program staff receives appropriate and required orientation and yearly education, and to comply with whatever requirements the parent organization promulgates. As recommended elsewhere, you will best be served by being able to produce copies of the parent organization documents immediately to show a surveyor. We offer under the above heading recommendations given earlier in the chapter relevant to staff education/orientation, written documentation, and staff discussion. You may find it advisable to review parent organization-wide expectations for your staff in a general emergency several weeks before your expected site visit. Independent of general parent organization preparation, you may want to convene a mock trial in some unit of your program. Of course, if you follow that suggestion, appropriate parties (e.g., organization CEO) should be informed of your plans.

All of your staff members need to be aware of procedures for use of particular equipment that may be dissimilar to equipment used in other settings. Most likely, such equipment will be limited to Breathalyzers. You will want to develop some system showing training for staff who have responsibility for using the instrumentation as part of your CQM program.

Table 8.3 Standards on Design and Implementation of the Environment of Care (EC.1 and EC.2) and Evidence of Compliance

Standards	*Evidence of Compliance*
• Create a safety management program. • Orient staff to reporting and investigating incidents. • Introduce the topic of safety into patient community meetings. • Have a plan to protect the security of your program environment. • Have accessible policies on handling hazardous materials and wastes. • Have accessible policies on emergency preparedness, life safety, and medical equipment.	• Policies and procedures memorandum that is available to staff and compatible with the parent organization's counterpart memorandum • Staff orientation publication • Copies of relevant performance plans that have a safety component • Minutes of clinical team staff meetings • Clinical records • Staff education and orientation materials • Clinical team staff meeting minutes showing attention to security matters • Copies of staff performance plans having a security element

Table 8.2 lists the key points included in discussion of safety standards on the design and implementation of the environment of care, and Table 8.3 lists major evidence that surveyors may use in evaluating the degree to which programs comply with these standards. Sources are linked to key points listed in Table 8.2.

To meet the measurement requirements of the standards, you need to assign a given staff member the role of program environment officer with ongoing responsibility for monitoring not only safety but also all other environmental factors of concern to Joint Commission surveyors. This staff member would be expected to engage in routine inspection of all areas in the SATP. Moreover, data gathered by the assigned individual would make a significant contribution to your CQM program. If relevant, you may want to tie your program's safety program more closely to your parent organization's program by having this staff member assigned as either a regular or an *ad hoc* member of the parent organization's safety committee. If such an assignment is not possible, we advise that your program environment officer receive the minutes of the organization's safety committee for monitoring of information pertinent to your program. If you have a freestanding SATP, Joint Commission standards suggest that you form a safety committee for the program itself.

Therapeutic Environment (EC.4)

In assessing the adequacy of your program's therapeutic environment, surveyors will be determining whether there is sufficient space; whether the environment fosters a positive self-image for the patients and preserves their human dignity; whether there is adequate privacy to reflect sensitivity and respect for patients; and whether there are activities to support the development and maintenance of patients' interests, skills, and opportunities for personal growth. We recommend that you ensure that your program setting is clean, well furnished, and not in need of paint or repair. We further suggest that you encourage patients to add personal touches to inpatient settings. These touches may include pictures, plants, or some collectable items. Take a critical walk to survey your entire space. Are magazines in the day rooms and waiting rooms up to date? If there are games available, are there missing pieces? If there is a piano, is it tuned? Are the overhead lighting fixtures clean? What repairs might be done to correct any problems? In some settings, such as therapeutic communities, patients may have responsibility for preparing and serving meals for other community members. In such a case, it is important that patients be educated about the need to maintain a clean meal preparation area and that dining areas be pleasant and conducive to social interaction (EC.4.9).

Programs in inpatient or residential contexts have available two standardized measures of program climate. The Ward Atmosphere Scale (WAS; Moos, 1989) was designed for use in inpatient settings, and the Community-Oriented Programs Environment Scale (COPES; Moos, 1988) was designed for use in residential settings. Both scales may be used to measure staff and patient perceptions of the therapeutic environment. Table 8.4 lists the three domains and 10 subscales that are measured by the WAS and the COPES. As shown in Table 8.4, the three domains and their respective subscales are the relationship domain, with subscales of Involvement, Support, and Spontaneity; the personal growth or treatment goal domain, with subscales of Autonomy, Practical Orientation, Personal Problem Orientation, and Anger and Aggression; and the system maintenance domain, with subscales of Order and Organization, Program Clarity, and Staff Control.

The WAS and the COPES have been used in multiple ways. For one, they have allowed some administrators to understand differences in how patients and staff view various aspects of the environment. For another,

Table 8.4   Domains and Subscales Measured by Both the Ward Atmosphere
Scale and the Community-Oriented Environment Scale

Domain	Subscales
Relationship	Involvement, Support, Spontaneity
Personal growth or treatment goal	Autonomy, Practical Orientation, Personal Problem Orientation, Anger and Aggression
System maintenance	Order and Organization, Program Clarity, Staff Control

Table 8.5   Standards for the Therapeutic Environment (EC.4)
and Corresponding Evidence of Compliance

Standard	Evidence of Compliance
Surveyors assess the adequacy of the therapeutic environment	Surveyor observation of program environment Written policy on smoking and the availability of smoking-cessation programs Use of standardized measures of environment perception as part of CQM efforts

they have been used to standardize the environment in some places where
ongoing research is important. Using the WAS or the COPES in this way
has allowed investigators to hold the treatment environment constant so
that results of various studies may be compared. Finally, the WAS and
the COPES have been used following some change in treatment to measure whether the desired effect was in fact attained. Table 8.5 presents
the key points about the therapeutic environment and corresponding
evidence that surveyors use to evaluate compliance with this standard.

Smoking Policy (EC.5)

Previously, criteria for a smoking policy were included under the
"social environment" standards. But in the current version of Joint

Commission standards, the smoking policy standard is grouped with standards concerning management of the environment of care. In this regard, surveyors will examine your policy on smoking. Be prepared to show any policy or written material you have on the topic. Identify areas, if any, outside of the building where patients can smoke. If you have resources for smoking-cessation treatment, make sure that you, your staff, and your patients can identify them.

Summary

Significant emphasis will be placed on your treatment environment by surveyors who will expect that it affords a safe, secure, clean, and pleasant social environment that is free of tobacco smoke. We have also recommended that you give one reliable staff member chief responsibility for monitoring the environment of your treatment site and that this individual be named to your parent organization's safety committee.

CHAPTER 9

Management of Human Resources

Elizabeth D. Brown
Paul P. Block

The work of human resource management is multifaceted and ongoing. It begins with identifying staffing requirements and goes on to recruitment, credential verification, orientation and ongoing training, and appraising performance. The Joint Commission expects that these activities occur in a work environment where management respects employees' rights and encourages employees' growth. A program is only as good as the employees it recruits and retains. In keeping with this philosophy, Joint Commission surveyors attend to how you utilize your staff resources. This chapter discusses the processes considered by the Joint Commission to be essential to human resource management. These include defining qualifications, competencies, and staffing needed to fulfill your program's mission; recruiting competent staff members or

141

Table 9.1   Key Points in Standards on Management of Human Resources

---

Human Resources Qualifications, Competencies, and Privileges
- Presence of multiple disciplines
- Description of specific model of goals and treatments to reach them
- Staff qualifications defined by patient characteristics and scope of problems in your patient population
- Evidence of licensing or certification; relevant education, training, and experience; and privileges or scope of practice for nonprivileged staff
- Definition of supervision required for performance of specific duties by different staff
- Treatment planners demonstrate specific qualifications
- Performance appraisal process in place, with objective criteria, regular renewal, and mechanisms for use in quality improvement and staff development

Orientation, Training, and Education of Staff
- Work atmosphere promotes staff development and learning.
- Orientation appropriately prepares staff to perform duties and maintain a safe environment.
- Ongoing education and training promote skill development for individual staff and across program staff as a whole.

Staff Rights Mechanisms
- Mechanisms exist for management of conflicts between job duties and staff values, including impact on patient care.

Competency Requirements for Special Populations
- Credentialing process and staff educational plan address special competency requirement for substance abuse work and, if applicable, for populations characterized by specific age groups, ethnicities, and/or sexual orientations.

---

negotiating contract services; generating and implementing a methodology for ensuring staff competence; and providing a work environment that promotes self-development and learning. Surveyors will use the performance improvement framework of the *MHM* (Joint Commission, 1995) in assessing your compliance with the human resources standards. Table 9.1 lists the key points in these standards, and Table 9.2 lists the sources that surveyors are likely to use in evaluating your SATP's compliance with these standards. You may want to refer to these tables as you read through the different sections of this chapter.

Table 9.2   Sources That Surveyors Might Use in Assessing SATP Programs'
Management of Human Resources

General Source
* Interviews with current staff or SATP leaders

Human Resources Qualifications, Competencies, and Privileges
* Written description of program treatment model and staffing plans
* Position descriptions or service contracts and performance standards
* Documentation about recruitment and hiring procedures
* Employee personnel files
* Performance appraisal plans and competence assessment mechanisms
* Policies on credentialing and privileging or scope of practice, including renewal procedures
* Peer review procedures

Orientation, Training, and Education of Staff
* Orientation curricula and records, including evaluations of individual staff performance on skills training or competency assessments
* Staff development plans
* In-service and continuing-education records, including needs assessments, agendas and outlines of specific training events, and attendance lists
* Minutes of staff meetings

Staff Rights Mechanisms
* Memoranda on identification and resolution of conflicts between staff duties and values, including mechanisms for ensuring appropriate patient care in such situations

Human Resources Qualifications, Competencies, and Privileges

Deciding How to Staff Your Program (HR.1, HR.1.1, and HR.1.2)

The *MHM*'s human resource standards require that you define the qualifications, competencies, and number of staff that you need to carry out your SATP programming. These qualifications and competencies must cover the care of special age and disability groups served in any of your settings. Further, your staff's qualifications must be sufficient for them to do the job duties that you expect to assign, and commensurate with licensure and certification.

Unless you are developing a new program, you may feel that the formal job of defining staffing represents the old saw of putting a horse in front of the preexisting cart. You are most likely dealing with a set number of staff who may have the protection of some kind of tenure earned through years of service or who may be under the aegis of a strong union. Still, defining the number and qualifications of staff need not be an empty exercise. Rather, it represents a chance for program tuning and for long-range planning. As an example, building staff strength in behavioral interventions was the long-term goal of one of the writers of this chapter. As opportunities presented themselves over the years, the program manager put the plan into action and created a strong cognitive-behavioral treatment program. We recommend that you assess your needs by determining the number, type, and qualifications of staff needed to work with your substance-abusing patients and their families. You may find little formal guidance available to you in decisions about the staff needed for the treatment team. How did you decide on the kind of staffing that you currently have? How might you change your planning for the future? We suggest, in keeping with the Joint Commission's requirement that treatment be delivered in a collaborative and interdisciplinary manner, that you consider an interdisciplinary team. We also recommend that you refer to your policy memoranda that address the assignment of responsibility to a certain professional or group of professionals for completing assessments, preparing treatment plans, and delivering care. You then can move on to determine how many staff you will need to deliver services to your patients. We advise that you start by identifying the desired qualifications for the core staff (e.g., psychiatrists, nurses, psychologists, social workers, and clerks). Then you can decide on what you need from other personnel involved in treatment or in maintaining a milieu characterized as psychotherapeutic and safe. In deliberating on staff qualifications, you will want to think about meeting patients' biopsychosocial needs. Other factors entering into staffing planning are your experience in working with your own patient population, your scrutiny of the MHM, and your evaluation of the needs of each program that is part of your SATP's continuum of care. In planning your care teams, you may note that the MHM mentions that full-time staff are useful for promoting trust and stability. The staffing patterns that allow such consistency are obviously preferable. We shall return to the topic of staff qualifications later in this chapter under the discussion of HR.5.

Once you have finished with the above deliberations, write or review position descriptions that delineate the expectations for job performance and the qualifications that each individual should bring to his or her position. Before moving on to other standards, we want to point out a secondary benefit for developing detailed position descriptions. In these times of downsizing, or in programs that have high staff turnover for whatever reasons, it is helpful to have descriptions of the specific treatment tasks. This material may help to justify your claims for appropriate staffing for your treatment program (and will not hurt in any internal discussions you might have about protecting your staff size). However, if your program does suffer staffing cuts, you should document the changes you plan in your treatment goals and in your model of treatment. Such changes reflect realistic expectations of the remaining staff and constitute additional evidence of compliance with HR.1.

Standard HR.1.1.1 mandates that staff members have sufficient expertise in working with special populations, here defined as age and disability groups. Note that there is a significant departure in these standards from those with which you may be familiar. Previously, the Joint Commission required a demonstration of knowledge about special populations only for nonprivileged clinical staff. Now the requirement exists for all staff, including the independent licensed clinicians (see HR.1.2). If your program serves special age or disabled groups, you will want to ensure that your staff are knowledgeable about the treatment and assessment needs for these groups. For example, if your program deals with addicted adolescents or with a substance-abusing geriatric population, your staff should have basic knowledge of the developmental factors associated with the patients' age group. In many settings, adolescent and even child substance abusers will make up the majority of patients. In other settings, staff may work with substance abusers' young families. When such activities take place, you also address staff competence with working with children or adolescents in hiring, in writing position descriptions, and in doing performance reviews. At the other end of the age span, we find an increasing number of geriatric patients in our medical settings. Here clinical staffs' position descriptions and performance plans address performance with the aging substance abuser. If you treat HIV-positive patients, staff must be well informed about the condition. We shall return to the issue of special populations as pertinent throughout this chapter.

In keeping with the intent of HR.1.1.2, Joint Commission survey-ors may seek confirmation that individual staff members' qualifications are commensurate with the job responsibilities described in their position descriptions. You will want to have files of appropriate licensure, certi-fication, or registration and indications of relevant education, training, and experience to show compliance.

The standards go on to address requirements for your clinical privileging of staff. To get a maximum score under HR.1.2, we recom-mend that you have credentialing files containing copies of current li-censing (when applicable), current clinical privileges or scope-of-practice determinations for nonprivileged staff, and educational/training and experience background in substance abuse treatments on hand. Verifica-tion of these factors should come from primary sources, which means that you need to contact schools, training programs, former employers, and licensing authorities for written evidence of qualifications. You cannot, for example, just use a photocopy of a diploma or license. To get a maximum score, these materials must appear in over 90% of the staff files. We also suggest that you keep relevant policy documents, reports, and minutes with the rest of your privileging materials.

Staff materials must include evidence of current competence and peer participation. You can show compliance with the former by having performance improvement data specific to the individual. The latter requirement can be met by review by your credentialing committee, by peer recommendations, or by formal peer review. If your staffing allows for it, you may want to be conservative in defining the term *peer*. Some agencies define peers as only those who have the same professional credentials. In these settings, a psychiatrist's peer can only be another psychiatrist; a social worker's peer can only be another social worker. We also recommend that you have continuing-education requirements relevant to substance abuse treatment for your staff. Ascertaining that these requirements have been met can be part of your review process.

We remind you that clinical privileges must be granted by profes-sional services or by the organization and renewed at least every 2 years. You should have on hand the written material describing credentialing/ privileging processes. This document should assign responsibility to organizational leaders for granting clinical privileges to independent providers. Moreover, you should have signed-off privileges on file to show that the leaders actually have approved privileges. As part of the document that defines privileging, you should address an appeals process. This description covers the scheduling of hearings, the procedures to be followed, the makeup of the hearing group, and the hearing's agenda. You also need to make sure that you have a mechanism for reviewing appeals fairly.

You should include functional statements and supervisory requirements in position descriptions of clinical staff members who do not have clinical privileges. This information should clarify these staff members' responsibilities and scope of practice. Although in some facilities, department heads rather than SATP leaders develop position descriptions for certain clinical staff, you should consult in the position description development to ensure that your program's criteria are met. Working from the position descriptions, you should then write or collaborate with department heads on writing performance plans for appraising employees' work. Finally, you and the relevant department heads need to develop and then employ procedures for using these plans in ongoing performance evaluation and quality improvement. If you are using contracted employees, you must similarly ensure that they are adequately supervised and that their competence is subjected to the same assessment process.

Staff Members' Competence (HR.2)

To demonstrate compliance with the standards in HR.2, you need to demonstrate that you have means for ongoing assessment, maintenance, and improvement of your staff members' competence. Here, once again, you can turn to evidence in performance appraisals, peer review systems, ongoing staff education, and leave time authorized for specialized educational opportunities. We recommend that you have staff members develop individualized development plans and that you think about having an ongoing educational series dedicated to substance abuse assessment and treatment.

We think of staff development as encompassing more than just educational growth. Staff also can and should develop personally to make a maximum contribution to patient care. The organizational psychology literature informs us that an individual staff member's growth is maximized in a work atmosphere compatible with individual development. This type of environment is completely congruous with continuous quality management concepts. Developing an atmosphere characterized by CQM is not a "one-shot deal." Rather, it requires a developmental process in which trust must first be established before employees can feel safe exposing their ideas and feelings. If staff are concerned about punishment for honest and open self-appraisal of their weaknesses, they will be much less likely to acknowledge areas for potential growth. On the other hand, if staff are rewarded for such reflections about how they can improve their performance, they are much more likely to commit to sincere self-development and learning.

Initially, the empowerment of SATP staff in the CQM process must come from upper-level management. In some organizations, this principle of empowerment may represent a distinct break from a long practice of autocratic, top-down leadership. Middle managers and clinical teams may have grown accustomed to their lack of flexibility in leadership. Moreover, the tradition of physicians as clinical leaders who are held responsible for the quality of treatment parallels the history of upper management's retaining decision-making power. These traditions often are long-lived and can be quite resistant to change. Many settings need outside consultation, along with considerable effort, to accomplish the significant shift in perceptions of responsibilities and authority that lead the team and upper management to empower the entire staff as a decision-making body.

Thorough and honest communication between you and your team members is a key element in initiating the process of empowerment. If your team is inappropriately empowered so that the range of its decision-making authority is not clear from the outset to all involved, the team may make decisions that are detrimental to other parts of the treatment system. For example, a team may decide that more office space is needed and that an unrelated treatment unit should forfeit space. In such cases, upper management may need to intervene. However much needed, and however well handled, the very process of such management interventions heightens mistrust and may sabotage the evolving CQM process. Thus it is critical that the empowerment process include clear and specific boundaries in defining the extent of the team's decision-making power.

Communication between upper-level management and team members also needs to be open and consistent. In many organizations, information is kept toward the top of the organizational structure. This practice may leave staff at lower levels feeling out of the communication loop and therefore not important to the organization. At other times, team members may have valuable information about day-to-day functioning of the program that could lead to important improvements in quality and efficiency. Team members may not communicate this information to management for a variety of reasons, including fear of coworkers' disapproval, resistance to change, or a conviction that management will not act on the information. Surveyors evaluate this standard through interviews, orientation curricula, and in-service or continuing education records, minutes, and reports.

Orientation, Training, and Education of Staff

Initial Job Training (HR.2.2)

Orientation, a Joint Commission requirement for *all* employees, provides an opportunity for an early assessment of staff members' capacity for performing their jobs, and it has the additional goal of acclimating individuals to a new job setting so that duties may be performed in a more effective and safe manner. In larger organizations, a distinct human resources service handles general orientation to the system as a whole; its norms, rules, and history; and the rights, responsibilities, and benefits for new employees. In addition to this orientation, your SATP should provide one of its own to introduce new staff to the program environment and to begin teaching the specialized needs for working with your patient population. Records should be kept showing that staff members have had both types of orientation. We also advise leaders to have on hand materials such as orientation syllabi, reports or minutes, staff evaluation of orientation, and policies dealing with orientation. Orientation records should include copies of any evaluations done of individual staff members' capability to perform to criterion specific duties for which they are receiving training either during orientation training or during any probationary period. Survey visitors also may choose to interview staff. If you use volunteer or contract workers in any level of your SATP programming, you should keep a record showing training for patient care and safety training equivalent to that of paid staff.

Ongoing In-Service and Other Education or Training (HR.2.3)

We recommend that you have on hand your program and plans for staff education, including ongoing training in treatments shown to work with substance-abusing patients. Several components may be in this material, such as individual development plans for staff, including explicit expectations for continuing education to be completed within defined time periods; requests for ordering relevant reading materials; a planned in-service educational curriculum; a collaborative education program with other programs or facilities; syllabi for training; and rosters showing names of staff who attended in-house educational offerings. For example, a large medical center might have an educational series sponsored by its staff education department that provides presentations for various critical topics in mental health. Working in collaboration with the education department, SATP staff would take responsibility for one of these meetings featuring risk management issues in treating substance abuse patients who are HIV-positive.

Regardless of the specific training needs of your staff, several issues should always be addressed in regular training. Because of the importance of HIV-positive status in substance-abusing populations, SATP staff should have ongoing training about implications and management of HIV and its medical and psychosocial effects. We advise you to keep records of each individual staff member's participation in continuing-education programming. All written materials relevant to staff education should be kept in an easily accessible folder.

Identification of Staff Learning Needs (HR.2.4)

We recommend that you engage in an ongoing effort with professional services or with members of different disciplines to collect information about staff training needs. For example, you can collect information from peer reviews, performance ratings, disciplinary actions, patient complaints, and patient gratitude letters. Once you have amassed this information for anonymity, the data can be studied as one determinant of staff learning needs. From this approach, you should be able to identify competency gaps to guide your planning for staff education. Individual training needs can also be identified by use of defined criteria for professional advancement. Grades within jobs, such as Addiction Therapist I, II, or III, should be based on training and demonstrated skills. As staff members reach a higher level of training and skill, you provide them with greater autonomy or increased scopes of practice. For this practice to succeed, you should define specifically what is needed for advancement. Your staff members then can use this definition in formulating their identified learning objectives. Regular feedback from patients, family members, or other members of your organization can also be important for identifying appropriate training goals.

Another means for educational planning involves needs assessment. One way to do such assessments easily is through E-mail if it is available at your treatment facility. You can keep responses on file to show surveyors how you established the need for education. You can also consult staff members' individualized development plans to determine educational needs. Learning about new developments in substance abuse work or new requirements of the Joint Commission also may lead you to plan new training. For example, if your program historically has worked primarily with alcohol abuse, a new influx of patients using injectable substances may require more staff training on HIV. You can initiate ongoing education within your program, or you may identify relevant learning occurring elsewhere. We suggest that you ascertain that training credited as fulfilling the SATP's ongoing education requirements is in fact relevant to working with substance abuse. For example, if a staff member attends a symposium on healthy child development, you should require the staff member to show that the course is applicable to the SATP setting. Suitable proof, in this instance, might be that the staff member has significant child contact in working with patients' families.

Competence Assessment (HR.3)

Although hiring competent staff may be the most important thing you do as an SATP leader, you will need to have processes in place for ensuring that your staff function in competent ways over time. In evaluating the performance appraisal system, surveyors expect to find performance plans written in objective terms with quantifiable results. We recommend that you work from the position description to cover all areas of the job in the plan and that you designate those elements of performance that are critical. The plan also details ongoing educational requirements and expectations for such things as maintaining safety in the SATP environment. You may be involved in developing these plans for a subset of the staff, most often addiction therapists, or for all of them, depending on the structure of your treatment facility. Performance appraisals for other staff members are often written by the department to which they are assigned if your treatment facility resides in a larger medical center. In this latter case, you should show a mechanism for informing performance raters about the staff member's work. If any staff work on a contractual basis, you should have on file a position description and a means for assessing performance and influencing outside evaluations.

You also may want to show evidence that you adjust performance plans as needed. You make such adjustments as an individual staff member gains new skills and gets new assignments or as your program changes and assignments become different. We suggest that you use self-appraisals from staff as further evidence of compliance with the standard. Other evidence of compliance can come from a formalized peer review system or from individual development programs.

The Joint Commission has separate specific standards for competence of staff who provide (or work on) child and adolescent services, mental retardation and developmental disabilities services, forensic services, and therapeutic foster care services. If any of these populations or activities characterize the focus of your program, you should also refer to these criteria in developing your competence assessment procedures. Surveyors base their scoring for HR.3 on the percentage of your staff members who have the competencies needed for working with your specific patient population. This competency assessment includes knowledge about the developmental issues associated with different age groups and with various disabilities represented. Although there are not specific standards for work with other special needs groups, the Joint Commission will expect that your staff are competent to work with the specific clinical features presented by the patients you serve. For instance, if you have deaf patients, you will be expected to have interpreters available, as well as staff or consultants with expertise in the cultural and functional implications of hearing impairment. Surveyors may look in a number of areas in assessing the HR.3 standard: staffing plans, position descriptions, service contracts, recruitment and hiring procedures, policies on privileging and credentialing, orientation curricula, memoranda on competency assessment mechanisms, employee personnel files, and interviews with current staff.

One way to ensure that you are in compliance is to require special privileges for work with children, adolescents, and geriatric patients if any of these groups is predominant in your treatment setting. Although it is not realistic to expect staff to be privileged for working with each different racial, ethnic, cultural, or religious group that your facility serves, competency assessment should include evaluation of staff members' understanding of individual and social differences that may influence treatment.

The Joint Commission also explicitly expects that you will have emergency response capabilities in place, including the availability at all times of staff who are trained in cardiopulmonary resuscitation (CPR). Further, you need to ensure that specifically designated staff stay current in emergency response certifications such as basic and advanced CPR training. For example, you might mandate CPR training for all clinicians, but not for your clerical staff. You also should note in writing who among your clinicians is exempt from the training—for example, a staff member who must use a wheelchair. In addition, you must train all staff for the responsibilities they might assume in various possible emergencies.

Staff Rights Mechanisms (HR.4)

Joint Commission standards on staff rights focus on the policies and mechanisms that you use in handling conflicts between care needs and staff values. You may need to make an assessment of patient care conditions that clash with caregivers' cultural values, ethics, or religious beliefs. In cases where such values do clash, you have two equal responsibilities. One responsibility is to enable the staff member to avoid engaging in activities that he or she personally opposes. The other responsibility is to ensure that the change in staff assignment does not adversely affect the patient's treatment. The Joint Commission expects specific policies and mechanisms to be in place for identifying such potential conflicts. This policy specifies how a staff member can request withdrawal from specific duties. The mechanism ensures that the necessary care remains available for patients.

In the context of substance abuse treatment, the most salient conflict clash might be in working with HIV-positive patients. A staff member might object on the grounds that a patient's medical status is related to his or her sexual orientation. You should take care in pre-employment interviews to inform applicants of the need to treat HIV-positive patients. If potential employees are unwilling to work with the patient population, we suggest that you not consider them for your program, but you may refer them elsewhere in the organization. If a staff member's unwillingness does not become known before he or she is in place, you may find value in providing education on precautions for infectious diseases in general and HIV in particular. Should the employee remain unwilling to work with HIV-positive patients, you should attempt to assign the staff member to a non-HIV-positive workload. If such an assignment leaves a patient without needed services, steps should be taken to reassign the staff member to a different unit of care, if possible, and to bring in a replacement.

Competency Requirements for Special Populations (HR.5)

In terms of establishing staff competence, you can begin to meet the *MHM*'s HR.5 standards by utilizing data from your organization's credentialing and privileging process. The Joint Commission requires that all licensed independent practitioners work under clinical privileges once these are evaluated and approved. However, the criteria exercised by professional departments in qualifications review are probably too general to satisfy completely the specialized competence needed to work in your program. You want to define for your program both the standards for judging competence and the requirements for ongoing professional education and supervision for the various types of personnel who are part of your staff. To accomplish this task, we recommend that you establish a written policy and procedure for conducting additional credentialing reviews. With such a process, you have a method for determining that staff members working in any of your programs have clearly established competence and experience in the field of substance abuse with the specific patients you serve. Newly hired professional staff who fail to meet your criteria should be closely supervised by appropriately

Table 9.3 Determining Competence for Substance Abuse Work (HR.5)

Clinicians who develop the summary and treatment must be able to

- Obtain information about and assess the relationship of each patient's physical status to the dependence, the nature of the patient's emotional compulsion to use alcohol and/or other drugs, and the intensity of the patient's mental preoccupation with using alcohol and/or other drugs
- Interpret information pertaining to an individual's use of alcohol and/or other drugs and develop a summary based on an established and recognized system
- Develop treatment plans based on patients' problems and needs

credentialed staff to gain sufficient experience to meet the credentialing criteria. Staff who provide care under supervision also need to be evaluated to ensure competency. Policies need to be in place describing the processes for evaluating competency, for determining appropriate scope of practice, and for defining the appropriate level of supervision for all supervised staff.

We strongly recommend that you be certain that any credentialing process conducted outside your program corresponds with any parent body's regulations (if relevant), your position description, and specific functional statements. For example, staff members without clinical privileges who provide group psychotherapy should have a functional statement in their position description authorizing the group work; psychologists doing neuropsychological evaluations should have that proficiency endorsed in privileges recommended by the psychology department, if relevant.

Surveyors expect those responsible for developing the diagnostic summary and for formulating treatment plans to demonstrate competence in obtaining and interpreting information about substance dependence (HR.5.1). Competence reviews of any of these staff should be explicit about credentials for performing treatment planning and delivery. Table 9.3 contains the elements on which your staff must demonstrate competence.

In particular, your staff's materials should reflect education, training, experience, and ongoing performance compatible with an ability to obtain, interpret, and apply information about substance dependence to develop an appropriate treatment plan. These staff must have objectively documented evidence of their knowledge of the natural history of dependence, including the ability to contrast the process and effects of substance dependence against other problems that might be confounded with the substance use disorder. This requirement means that these staff understand the biological and sociocultural influences on substance dependence.

Your staff also should have a general understanding of the range of treatment needed by substance-dependent patients and knowledge of available treatment resources and their appropriate utilization. Furthermore, you should have evidence showing that staff can and do differentiate treatment needs on the basis of the acuity or chronicity of the addiction. More specifically, it would be helpful to define the specific treatments that you believe are required to fulfill your program's therapeutic goals and then to define the particular skills that your staff need as a group to be able to conduct these treatments adequately. Surveyors will appreciate this clarity in your definition of staff expectations.

Treatment planners need a general understanding of the range and level of treatments available and their appropriate use, including those available at your particular facility and at other facilities that might be able to offer services to patients who cannot be adequately treated in your program. These competencies should be demonstrated through ongoing quality measurement and improvement activities focused on the treatment-planning process in particular.

Good practice would indicate that you ensure that all of your staff have both didactic training and supervised experience in specialized treatments that have documented evidence of success with substance abusers. For instance, you should have staff with documented skills in cognitive-behavioral treatments for addictions, including relapse prevention training. Other therapeutic approaches with evidence of usefulness include behavioral marital therapy, community reinforcement, and motivational interviewing (Miller & Rollnick, 1991).

Summary

Management of human resources ranges from the definition of the staff qualifications needed to fulfill specific treatment roles, through recruitment and hiring, training, and performance appraisal, to the management of staff performance and staff development. Surveyors will look for clearly documented rationales for your handling of each of these steps. They also will expect that you use objective criteria in evaluating staff at all steps of this management continuum. We have posited that the best justification of your decision-making policies and procedures at each of these steps rests on an explicit definition of (a) the goals your program hopes to achieve, (b) the model of intervention you use to reach those goals, and (c) the specific staff activities required to implement the relevant interventions in effective ways for your specific patient population and setting. This tri-partite definition allows clear understanding of the staff qualifications required, effective division of responsibilities, relevant staff development, and necessary monitoring and evaluation of staff performance. We have also advocated that you pay particular attention to ensuring that your staff's training and experience include approaches shown to be effective in the treatment outcome literature.

Your surveyor will examine your staff members' qualifications to work with different populations. Credentialing and privileging processes are particularly important in the Joint Commission criteria for licensed, independent care providers. We have addressed your need to have in place other mechanisms for determining competence of nonprivileged, supervised staff.

We have also provided discussion on handling standards dealing with conflicts between staff values and assigned duties. Finally, we have emphasized how critical it is that your environment encourage and reward honest self-appraisal and self-development on the part of all staff, rather than punishing disclosures of any areas needing growth.

CHAPTER 10

Management of Information

Elizabeth D. Brown
Stephen F. Gibson

Management-of-information standards cover a wide range of activities, some more relevant than others in the local treatment setting. The Joint Commission requirements on management of information previously had little direct bearing on survey visits to the treatment unit itself other than the obvious requirement that staff follow certain practices in recording patient information. With the new comprehensive standards in the *MHM* (Joint Commission, 1995), substance abuse treatment staff need to be much more involved in designing, maintaining, and using information management systems. In this chapter we address how your staff can have and should have input into the design or operation of whatever system you develop to generate and use information.

To meet Joint Commission standards, information management design requirements must meet internal and external needs. Often an administrative department generates the design and implementation of the information management plan. This outcome is most likely to occur when the clinical program is embedded in some larger structure, such as a medical center. In such cases you should provide the planning group with information about your treatment program's needs, including hardware needs.

In rarer instances the clinical program may have more of a free-standing status. Here you may have direct responsibility for the assessment of information management needs. You may need to design the information management system on the basis of your assessed needs. Moreover, you may need to maintain the system and decide on the appropriate use of information derived from it. We say more on this topic in the section "Knowledge Needs for Staff."

We are assuming a somewhat different orientation than does the *MHM* in dealing with the topic of information management. This chapter redirects the material in a way that should be more useful to staff actually involved in patient care. As such, we have chosen to group the standards differently and not necessarily in the same order as the *MHM*. To assist the reader who is trying to cross-reference the material, each heading throughout the chapter identifies the standard being addressed. Table 10.1 presents the format used in the chapter.

The chapter begins by addressing the usefulness of information for patient care needs. The Joint Commission addresses assessment and design of the information management process in the IM.1 standards. We also discuss what should be done to maximize the timeliness, completeness, and accuracy of material that is in the record, standards presented in the *MHM* under IM.7. Not so long ago, a demonstration of ready access to a well-done and complete and timely patient file would have satisfied surveyors. In today's world, the computer has gained ascendancy, giving many of us the electronic record. With this new capacity, more efficiency has been realized with staff's ability to access and enter information into the record from remote sites and with greater speed. Recognizing that not all treatment programs are at the same stage in their use of technology, the Joint Commission has developed its standards for data management in a manner that allows application to settings that are far advanced and to others in which little has been done.

Table 10.1 Key Points in Addressing Management of Information

Usefulness of Information for Patient Care Needs

- Assessing/planning/designing an adequate information management system for patient care
- Timeliness, completeness, and accuracy of recording

Access to Information

- Security of records
- Timeliness in information dissemination and/or transmission

System Uses for Information

- Assessing/planning/designing an adequate information management system for program decision making
- Standardization
- Linkages between patient care information and organizational databases
- Ability to aggregate information for organization decision making
- Access to external data for comparison purposes

Knowledge Needs of Staff

- Expertise in managing, retrieving, and analyzing information
- Access by clinical staff to relevant professional literature

Nonetheless, programs that are fortunate enough to have computerized records may find it easier to show compliance with survey criteria.

Next, we move to the issues related to access of information. For this topic, we provide information about timeliness in information distribution and transmission (IM.6). We further discuss the importance of security of records (IM.2). The third section of the chapter presents material about systems' use of information. Here we first speak to the organization's assessment of its program needs in information management (IM.1) and to the standardized processes it needs to define and collect data (IM.3). We then move to the topic of linking various databases as needed for organizational decision making (IM.6). These databases may include data internal to the organization and external to it; they may consist of clinical data and administrative data. We then approach aggregation of data, an integral step in using any database for systems-level decision making (IM.8.) This section ends with standards on access to external databases for comparing your program's perfor-

Table 10.2   Standards Related to Usefulness of Patient Records and Evidence
of Compliance

Standards	Evidence of Compliance
Assessing/designing the information management system (IM.1)	Clinical team minutes Memoranda/reports on assessed needs Staff representation on information management committees Staff interviews Evidence that the organization has supplied resources in response to requests
Quality and timeliness of patient records (IM.7)	Policies and procedures Review of clinical records Minutes from clinical team meetings CQM data on record reviews Staff interviews Attendance records and syllabi from in-service education

mance against that of substance abuse programs in other settings (IM.10).
Toward the end of the chapter, we introduce standards related to staff
knowledge. In this section we deal with the expertise needed to develop,
maintain, and use information management systems (IM.4) and the
mechanisms necessary for clinical staff's ready access to recent professional literature (IM.9).

Usefulness of Information

Table 10.2 provides an overview of what surveyors look for under
the *MHM* headings IM.1 and IM.2. These standards pertain to the
usefulness of information. We also provide in the table a listing of some
materials you may want to have available to show that your staff members
understand and have met the standards.

Assessing/Designing an Information Management
System Within SATPs (IM.1)

Surveyors will expect an integrated system of information management that is usable both for quality patient care and for organizational

or program decision making. The chapter addresses the latter topic in the section "Systems Uses for Information." The standard's intent is threefold. First, surveyors want to ensure that there has been careful thought about the types of information needed to deliver good patient care. Second, they will expect that you have assessed the outcome of that care. Third, they will want to see how you use the system to make programmatic decisions. In determining how complex your information management system should be, you will need to consider a variety of topics, including your program's mission and goals, your patient population, the types of services you provide, your resources, and issues of access. Your staff may collect needs assessment information experientially or by a more formal data-gathering process. You should reflect discussion of needs in your program's minutes. Should a representative of another department come to an SATP meeting to discuss your needs for data management, minutes should capture that event as well.

The design of information management systems should be a collaborative effort between clinical and administrative staff. Clinicians know best what information they need for high-quality clinical care; administrative personnel may be more adept at developing/maintaining the technology necessary to capture information efficiently. For example, you may develop a template that, if computerized, would greatly speed up patient assessments. However, to have this template installed into the computer system, you may have to call on administrative staff's expertise. As another example, if your program is part of a larger system of care or has multiple sites, needs assessment may show that clinicians at one program are having trouble getting records signed out to another site. Administrative staff intervention may provide a solution by having multi-site access to an electronic record or by having better retrieval and forwarding of a hard-copy record.

Along with all of its advantages, the introduction of the electronic record may require assessment of staff needs. At the beginning stages of using the electronic record, you may find considerable staff resistance to it. It has been our experience that much of the reluctance comes from two factors. First, staff members resist more if they do not have immediate access to a terminal. You may find more compliance if there are multiple terminals and, in particular, terminals in staff members' offices. If you assess this need at your site, you can inform the data-processing department that you need more terminals. An account of this action can be kept as evidence to surveyors that assessment has been done in improving the information management system.

Second, we have found that many staff who are used to dictating or manually writing in a chart have never developed good typing skills. For these staff who dread learning how to use electronic equipment, record entries initially will consume more time. If you encounter this kind of problem, your needs assessment may lead you to request educational modules on typing skills. We recommend that you keep evidence that you requested the training and that the organization responded to your request. Other assessments may show patient-related needs (e.g., computerized testing requiring additional terminals for patient access) or organizational reporting needs. Once you have identified these needs, you should submit them to the appropriate group in a report. These reports, also, can be kept together as part of your documentation for surveyors.

Besides meeting standards that are directly applicable to the clinical setting, we recommend that you keep informed about where any parent organization is moving with information management. We suggest that you invite representatives of administrative departments at regular intervals to your staff meetings. These personnel can keep you and your staff informed about developments in data management, patient billing, utilization review, and other relevant topics.

Timeliness, Completeness, and Accuracy of Recording (IM.7)

Joint Commission standards are very explicit about the need for timeliness, completeness, and accuracy of recording. We recommend that you keep an updated policy and procedure memorandum specifying the types of material that staff should enter into the record, the timing for the entry, and the designation of staff authorized to make entries. If you have a multi-partite program (e.g., inpatient detoxification, partial hospitalization, outpatient rehabilitation, and specialty programs), the memorandum should be comprehensive enough to cover all levels of programming. We further suggest that you have a memorandum outlining a CQM process for record monitoring. Here again we suggest that you specify the types of staff, at least some of whom should be your clinicians, responsible for the work. You also need to state the requirement that such monitoring occur at least on a quarterly basis on a significant number of representative records. The focus of the review is on whether records accurately reflect the patient's diagnosis, diagnostic tests, therapy, condition, in-hospital progress, and condition on discharge. Moreover, there should be a judgment about the timeliness of entries and whether patients received a full range of services. Your leadership staff can build other relevant parameters into the review. You might consider developing a scoring form containing each element listed under IM.7.2 and attaching this form to the memorandum. In that the Joint Commission makes no distinction between outpatient and inpatient programming in terms of type of information charted, you can use the same form for all levels of the care you provide. We suggest that you incorporate this quarterly monitoring as part of your organizational improvement focus. When you find unacceptable recording practices, you can report the problem, develop a solution, and improve. You will also want to show that you cover record-keeping requirements in orientation, in-service education, and staff meetings.

You can use a similar process to show that discharge and transfer summaries have all of the necessary elements listed under IM.7.3. Here you will be concerned with documentation stating

1. The reason for treatment
2. The significant findings
3. The procedures done and the treatment given
4. The patient's condition on discharge and any specific directions relayed to the patient and the patient's family

In IM.7.5 the standards require that you compile a summary sheet of treatment-related information by the third visit for patients in outpatient or partial-hospitalization programs.

This listing must be kept current for those patients who have a longer course of treatment. Among the elements that surveyors address here are

1. Assessment-derived material about past significant courses of treatment
2. Past and current diagnoses or problems
3. Assessment-derived information about adverse and allergic drug reactions
4. Currently and recently used medications

We recommend that assessments and treatment plans for patients discharged to an outpatient program following inpatient care reflect the problems noted and the inpatient treatment plan. In particular, these plans must address the reassessment of problems for which treatment was deferred or not completed during the inpatient stay.

IM.7.6 focuses on the timing for record entries. The physical examination and history need to be completed within 24 hours of a patient's admission, with no exceptions for weekends and holidays. However, if there is a report of a physical examination done within the last 30 days, you may omit a new examination. Of course, if the patient's condition has changed in the 30-day period, you will want to have a new examination done. For inpatient readmissions within 30 days of discharge, you need only a three-part process. First, you will do an interval history and physical report acknowledging that you have reviewed the previous history and physical examination. Second, you either specify pertinent additions to the history and/or subsequent changes in the physical findings or say that there has been no change. Third, you keep the results of the examination from the previous admission in the record.

In residential settings, you need to enter physical examination results into patient records within 7 days. There is no clearly stated expectation for completion of an examination for outpatient and partial-hospitalization care; you decide on the need for a physical examination on the basis of your screening. Patients' records must be complete by 30 days post-discharge. The *MHM* also says that you should update treatment plans to reflect changes in patients' needs and response to treatment change. However, the standards do not address a specific time for treatment planning for the patient who continues in care with little change. We believe that treatment planning should be an ongoing process. Treatment planning is discussed in depth in Chapter 4 of this book.

Surveyors also will want to know how you allow only qualified staff members to take verbal orders from other staff authorized to give such orders (IM.7.7). We recommend that you identify these staff by job title in a policy and procedure document. This document must also require that there be physician input for orders that may present any danger to patients. Further, it must address the need for signing off on verbal orders within a specified time period. If you have access to medical center guidelines on this topic, you will want to keep a copy of this policy in easy reach of staff. If a policy does not exist, we advise that you produce one. Besides wanting to see the policy, surveyors doing record reviews will evaluate whether staff members follow the policy. Finally, you need to be able to show that your clinical staff members have a definition for verbal orders that carry any element of risk to patients. We strongly recommend that your staff minutes reflect discussion on this last requirement. We also suggest that you have an ongoing mechanism to sensitize remaining and new staff to verbal orders that may be associated with risk.

MHM standards under IM.7.8 focus on the dating and signing off of entries into the clinical records. These standards also address the identification of your staff who enter material into the record. Staff must date and authenticate all entries in your patients' records. Authentication can consist of signatures, computer sign-offs (for electronic records), or rubberized signature stamps. Staff using either of the last two options need to sign a statement acknowledging that they will not allow anyone else to use the personalized computerized sign-off or stamp. These statements should be kept on file. Staff also must know that only they can sign off on a computerized record for which they have responsibility. In showing that you meet these standards, you will want to produce policy material generated either by your program or by any parent organization. You may want to bring up the matter in team meetings to keep staff up to date. You surely will want to monitor the process of sign-offs in your record reviews. Remember that surveyors also may look at dating of material during record reviews. The survey team also may talk to staff about dating and authenticating.

We suggest that you designate formally which signatures need countersigning. You must require countersigning for notes by house staff or other trainees. If your program is part of a larger health structure, you need to read that parent organization's bylaws to learn which, if any, nonphysician staff need to have their work countersigned. For example, a registered nurse usually must countersign admission nursing notes written by a nursing assistant or licensed practical nurse. Once you have made this determination, you should incorporate the information into whatever local policy memorandum exists on the subject.

The clinical data and information standards (IM.7) conclude with clinicians' access to records—their own and those of clinicians in other parts of the medical/rehabilitation setting—for both scheduled and un-

Table 10.3   Demonstrating Compliance With Record Keeping (IM.7)

Completeness of record (IM.7)

Clinical record entries are made only by authorized personnel (IM.7.1.1)

Completeness of transfer/discharge summaries (IM.7.3)

Complete summary list for partial hospitalization/outpatient patients within 3 days (IM.7.5)

Timeliness of record entries (IM.7.6)

Dealing with verbal orders (IM.7.7)

Record entries are dated and authenticated; means for identifying entry writers exist (IM.7.8)

Complete records are available for scheduled and unscheduled visits (IM.7.9)

A process exists to inform authorized personnel if part of the record is filed elsewhere (IM.7.9.1)

---

scheduled visits. If your program has moved to the electronic record, you can probably show that you have met the standard (IM.7.9). If you rely on the hard-copy record, you may want to gather data to assess whether you are in compliance. You need to show that you have met the standards in at least 91% of the records to get a maximum score. In some settings, particularly those where patients receive services at different geographic sites, meeting this standard without computerized records presents considerable difficulty. Should your survey of record availability reveal problems, you may choose to incorporate the problem as part of your continuing improvement efforts. You should write up improvements that you have made as part of your compliance file.

If it is appropriate to your setting, you also should adopt some system for handling the issue of multiple parts of the medical record stored at various sites. Clinicians will need some means for knowing that other relevant material may be stored. You might want to copy pertinent material from such files to incorporate it into the files that your clinicians use.

We recommend that you review your policy and procedure memoranda and evidence of compliance several weeks before the survey visit for the categories listed in Table 10.3. For each category you should identify the policy number and/or written evidence of compliance. We advise that you assemble these materials in an organized fashion so that you can readily answer surveyor questions by retrieving the data.

Table 10.4 Access to Information Standards and Evidence of Compliance

Standards	Evidence of Compliance
Timeliness in information dissemination and/or transmission (IM.5)	Policy/procedure memoranda Staff interviews CQM data Access to electronic technology
Security of records (IM.2)	Observation Approved codebooks Minutes from meetings Policy/procedure memoranda Staff interviews Observations Records of action taken on discovering violations Minutes from staff meetings Syllabi and attendance sheets from orientation sessions

Access to Information

The Joint Commission has standards not only about accessing patient records specifically but also about accessing data in general, including data not directly related to patient care. Moreover, surveyors expect you to use standardized terminology and format in generating or distributing information. Table 10.4 presents these standards and evidence of compliance with them.

Timeliness in Information Dissemination and/or Transmission (IM.5)

Standards in IM.5 assess whether transmission of data and information is timely and accurate and whether you are using a standardized format and method for data dissemination. The standards subsume a vast array of information. Does your program get prompt turn-around on laboratory testing? Does one unit in your continuum of care give prompt decisions to another unit about the appropriateness of a patient transfer? Do dietary orders get timely attention? Are data, including those not directly related to patient care, transmitted accurately? Surveyors assessing the standards may examine medical center (if relevant) and program policies and procedures, and they may interview staff. Your ability to display electronic advances to increase access to clinically relevant material will be advantageous. We recommend that you show use of the electronic record, voice mail for receiving messages about findings, and/or E-mail used to facilitate information retrieval.

A standardized format and method for disseminating data and clinical material also fall under IM.5. You may want to use some meeting time to clarify that your staff members are using standardized terminology in their understanding of patient care. This approach also feeds into the process of ongoing staff education. For example, one of the writers for this chapter recently was in a group where there was a lively discussion about distinctions among a "clinical pathway," a "critical pathway," and "clinical guidelines." Before arriving at a consensus the group gained a great deal of educational information.

We advise that you learn if your staff members have problems in retrieving specific material and if standardization is a problem in your setting. If difficulties are found, you can take remedial action. This advice may be especially important if your treatment setting does not have the advances cited above. In addressing criteria under the IM.5 heading, you want to be sure that a policy memorandum covers the means for transmission of data. This coverage may be in a policy memorandum generated by any parent organization. If your treatment program is freestanding, you should write your own policy document.

Security of Records (IM.2)

We addressed the topic of confidentiality in Chapter 1 of this book. Other relevant information is in Chapter 3. Standards in the *MHM*'s IM.2 focus more on the tangible information related to treatment, whereas earlier discussion also covered the intangible, such as conversations in the cafeteria. In those instances we recommended that you bring up the need for patient confidentiality in staff orientation. We also suggested that you keep materials on the need for confidentiality visible throughout the SATP. We similarly recommend an orientation and educational focus on the need for securing data.

We suggest that you assemble copies of policies and procedures on the need to keep data secure. You can use this material as part of the educational packets that you make up for your staff. The policy statements and training should cover all six elements of security listed in Table 10.5.

Table 10.5   Elements Addressed in Securing Information

Define who has access to information.

Denote the types of information an individual can access.

Delineate the obligation of the individual who has access to information to keep it confidential.

Designate the mechanisms for release of health information and/or removal of the clinical record.

Depict the mechanism designed to secure information against loss, destruction, unauthorized intrusion or use, corruption, and damage.

Describe the process to use when confidentiality and security may be violated.

Staff training should stress that the release of any patient information must be done only by authorized persons and only to authorized persons. Staff training also should cover the need for security of hard copies of records. In particular, staff should know that areas for record storage are kept locked unless a staff member is in that area. During training, program leaders should instruct staff members who have access to any computerized patient information that they must not give their access and verify codes to other individuals. Should there be a need to have patients transport their "hard" record to a clinic or another setting, staff should place the record in a locked bag.

You can produce staff minutes or orientation/training syllabi to show that you have informed staff members about the need for security. We also recommend that you insert a copy of the medical center's policy on confidentiality into a loose-leaf binder with copies of other policy memoranda that are relevant to the SATP. Joint Commission surveyors may interview staff and make observations to evaluate compliance with the standard.

Systems Uses for Information

In Table 10.6 we list main points covered in the *MHM*'s categories IM.3, IM.6, IM.8, and IM.10. We also include some information pertinent to IM.1. Our previous discussion of IM.1 focused on developing an information system from the perspective of information needs for patients' direct care. Now we shall address the topic from the vantage point

Table 10.6 Standards Related to Organization Needs for Information in
Decision Making and Evidence of Compliance

Standards	*Evidence of Compliance*
Assessing/designing an information management program on a systems level (IM.1)	Minutes from meetings Reports Staff interviews Program changes made in response to information Needs assessments
Standardization (IM.3)	Policy and procedures Use of *DSM-IV* in discharge summaries Lists of definitions and approved abbreviations Staff interviews Record reviews
Database linkages (IM.6)	Policies and procedures Utilization review reports Outcome evaluation reports Staff interviews Reports on referral patterns Changes in patient care practice in response to data-based CQM
Information aggregation for organizational decision making	Policies and procedures Staff interviews Reports using aggregate data (IM.8) Changes in patient care practice in response to aggregate data-based CQM
External versus internal comparisons (IM.10)	Policies and procedures Staff interviews Reports showing comparisons Staff meeting minutes discussing comparisons

of the types of information needed for organizational or program decision making. Here we think of the standards as pertaining to the usefulness of information. As in other sections of this book, we also list some sources that you may use to show compliance with standards.

Assessing/Designing an Information Management
Program on a Systems Level (IM.1)

If your program is part of a larger medical care setting, you most
likely will not bear the chief responsibility for assessing informational
needs and designing a data management program congruent with your
needs. Even here, however, you should assess the kinds of data that would
be useful for running your program. For example, you will need outcome evaluation data. What information might your organization's data-
capturing system provide for you for evaluative studies? You also need
to think about how to interface with the larger organization's information management staff. If there is a committee associated with data gathering, can one of your staff members become a member of it? Do you
have a liaison with the information management department? Are representatives from the information management department regularly in-
vited to your staff meetings to discuss needs, problems, or developments?

If, on the other hand, your program is not a subunit of a larger
medical organization, you and your staff should do a complete assessment of the types of information needed. You might also find that you
need some staff members who are expert in computer technology. These
staff would be responsible for designing and operating the data capture
mechanism. You would also expect them to keep your system updated
for new types of information that you may need. The remarks made
earlier about assessing and designing an information management system
for patient care needs are pertinent to the tasks in front of you.

Standardization (IM.3)

In the *MHM*'s IM.3, the Joint Commission intends to assess your
use of standardized terminology. Surveyors will want to know if you can
compare your care with care provided at other treatment settings that
use the same terminology. Thus, as you think about the definitions that
you use in describing clinical phenomena or in collecting data, you need
to rely on commonly used definitions and classification strategies. Besides examining policy memoranda addressing the use of standard terminology, surveyors will expect that only officially sanctioned abbrevia-
tions appear in patient charts.

IM.3.2 covers quality control systems to monitor data collection so
that data sets are valid, efficiently assembled, and produced in a cost-
effective manner. You should have someone available during the site visit
who is familiar with data validation relevant to your program. Similarly,
if your treatment setting is embedded in some larger organization with
a medical records committee, staff should be able to describe interactions
with committee members.

Standardization may also be important from a reimbursement
perspective. For example, we have had the experience of standardizing
visit codes, a need made evident when we tried to compare various years'
workloads. Some clinicians were listing visits under alcohol codes, others
under drug treatment codes, and still others under substance abuse codes.
In an attempt to promote uniformity of reporting, leaders met with administrative staff to review each clinical staff person's reporting. During
this meeting, we discovered that staff had coded visits to one program in
a manner not recognized by the hospital's computer system. Data from
that program had not been reported for an unknown period of time, and
the medical center had never been reimbursed for the patient workload.
When such an event occurs, you should reflect it in minutes, reports, and
perhaps in CQM findings.

Standards IM.3.3.1 and IM.3.3.2 concern the monitoring of patient records for presence, accuracy, and timely recording of information,
as well as the authentication of the data. For purposes of this chapter,
these standards are redundant; we presented everything needed to meet
these standards earlier in the chapter. The reader may refer to the section
"Usefulness of Information." The type of at least quarterly monitoring
recommended there should allow you to show perfect compliance with
the standards.

Linkages Between Patient Care Information
and Organizational Databases (IM.6)

You should know about any policies that govern your treatment
setting's storage and use of clinical records for compliance with IM.6.1.
If your program is not freestanding, some department in the administrative side of your organization may have already produced this policy and
may be ensuring compliance with it. On the other hand, if you are
working in an independent site, you may be the individual who has to

Table 10.7 Points to Address in Use of Databases

Specify length of time for information retention.

Ensure that specified storage time is congruent with relevant laws and regulations.

Note how data can be used for care delivery.

Stipulate use of data for legal purposes.

State conditions for using databases for research.

State conditions for using databases for education.

---

ensure that the policy is written and followed. Should this be the case, the policy that you develop must say how long you will store materials. This policy must be compatible with state or federal (for federal facilities) laws and regulations. Further, this policy should specify the use of the case material for treatment purposes, legal matters, research endeavors, or educational programs. Table 10.7 lists the six components that surveyors will expect you to handle in your policy. Moreover, in that surveyors may also want to check on whether you manage databases as described in your policy, we recommend that staff who are involved in the gathering, analysis, and utilization of these data be available during the site visit to answer any surveyor questioning about the degree to which they follow the written policy.

Aggregating Information for Organization Decision Making (IM.8)

Standards under IM.8 cover some of the topics for which medical centers and treatment programs need to aggregate data for an overall assessment. The topics covered in the standards range from oversight of prescription practices to safety issues and to the use of aggregated data for performance improvement and decision making. An example of how data can be aggregated for decision making is in Figure 10.1. This graph shows that elderly patients absorbed most of the clinical resources for acute medicine but that this population used few treatment resources in the medical center's substance abuse and psychiatry programming. With such data, program leaders can study several important questions. Do elders have no treatment needs? Is the program failing in its identification and outreach to elders? Or might elders with treatment needs be unwilling to enter treatment?

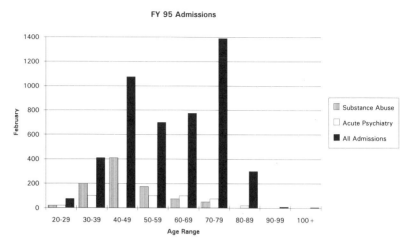

Figure 10.1. Graph Using Aggregated Data to Assess Differential Usage of Treatment Resources by Elder and Younger Patients

Other uses for data aggregation also have direct program pertinence. For example, combined data can allow you to assess trends in utilization of your resources. Thus you might want to examine length of stay in inpatient programs or length of treatment in outpatient care.

If your treatment program is part of a larger medical setting, you may already have many of the resources on hand to be in compliance with standards related to combined data sets. For example, you may have ready access to a computer department, a medical records department, a pharmacy committee, a safety committee, a risk manager, and an infection control committee. In these cases, the medical center may have established policy on relevant topics. We suggest that you review such documents so that you are knowledgeable about their contents. If you find that the policy is not congruent with the needs of your program, we recommend that you work with the department that issued the document on any revisions needed.

On the other hand, if your program does not have the resources listed above, you will have the responsibility for developing the background materials, education, and processes for gathering and amalgamating data in an accurate, timely, and cost-effective manner. The areas you should address are presented below in three tables. Table 10.8 lists the components that surveyors will assess in evaluating how you aggregate

Table 10.8 Standards for Aggregating Data on Medication Practices and Evidence of Compliance

Standards	*Evidence of Compliance*
Control and accountability of all drugs at an on-site pharmacy (IM.8.1.1.1)	Policies and procedure Reports Minutes from pharmacy committee meetings (if you have one) Reports Staff interviews
Identifying signatures of all clinicians authorized to prescribe or order medication (IM.8.1.1.2)	On-file list of signatures Minutes from pharmacy committee meetings Staff interviews
A listing of clinicians' Drug Enforcement Administration numbers when required (IM.8.1.1.3)	Listing of Drug Enforcement Administration workers

Table 10.9 Aggregating Data on Safety/Hazards and Evidence of Compliance

Standards	*Evidence of Compliance*
Problems associated with safety management, life safety management, equipment management, and utilities management (IM.8.1.2.1)	Reports Safety committee minutes Staff meeting minutes Staff interviews Orientation syllabi
Relevant published reports of hazards associated with safety management, life safety management, equipment management, and utilities management (IM.8.1.2.1)	Posted articles Warnings on E-mail Staff interviews Safety committee meeting minutes
Semiannual surveys of all areas to identify environmental hazards and unsafe practices (IM.8.1.2.2)	Reports from survey Evidence of corrective action Staff interviews Staff meeting minutes Safety committee meeting minutes
Dealing with property damage, occupational illness, or patient, staff, or visitor injury (IM.8.1.2.3)	Administrative reports Investigative reports Evidence of corrective action Safety committee meeting minutes Policy regarding critical incident stress debriefing (if you have adopted CISD)

Table 10.10 Standards for Data Aggregation for Problem Detection, Reporting, and Organizational Decision Making and Evidence of Compliance

Standards	*Evidence of Compliance*
Required reporting to proper authorities (IM.8.1.3)	Reports Staff interviews
Coding and retrieval system for clinical records by diagnosis and procedure (IM.8.1.4)	Reports Staff interviews Demonstration of computer system
Coding and retrieval system for patient demographic information (IM.8.1.5)	Reports Staff interviews Demonstration of computer system
Coding and retrieval system for financial information (IM.8.1.6)	Reports Staff interviews Demonstration of computer system
Measures of processes and outcomes for assessing performance (IM.8.1.7)	Program evaluation material Reports Staff interviews
Actions taken on problems uncovered in the areas of risk management, utilization management, infection control, and safety management (IM.8.1.8)	Reports Evidence of corrective action Staff education syllabi Changes in staff orientation material Staff interviews Staff meeting minutes Safety committee minutes Relevant E-mail
Accurate and timely information for operational decision making and planning (IM.8.1.9)	Reports Programmatic changes made based on data Staff interviews
Data and information to support clinical research, as desired (IM.8.1.10)	Staff interviews Professional papers/professional presentations based on data

data pertinent to medication prescription (IM.8.1.1). Table 10.9 catalogs the information dealing with aggregating information about safety (IM.8.1.2). Table 10.10 lists the remaining areas that may be of interest to surveyors.

Access to External Data for Comparison Purposes (IM.10)

The *MHM*'s standards on using external data evolve from the belief that you can use such data in organizational improvement, including the detection of undesirable practice patterns. The standards contain just three elements. First, your medical center or your program needs access to an external database that is based on national and/or state guidelines. Scoring guidelines for IM.10 suggest a number of areas that you might tap for the data. Second, surveyors will assess whether you are contributing comparative data to at least one external database that, in turn, is providing you data. Third, you will need a system for ensuring the security and confidentiality of data that you are receiving or submitting. To meet these standards, you should make certain that you have a policy and procedure document laying out the means for protecting security and confidentiality. Earlier, we recommended a similar document for securing your in-house information. To avoid redundant memoranda, you can add a section on the handling of external data to your already-existing memorandum. Surveyors will assess your compliance with IM.10 by staff interviews and by letters of agreement with external data providers. If you have reports with conclusions based on external data or can point to programmatic decisions made on the basis of such data, these materials should be kept on hand.

Knowledge Needs for Staff

Expertise in Managing, Retrieving, and
Analyzing Information (IM.4)

Standards under the IM.4 heading require that decision makers who generate, collect, and analyze data know what they are doing with data management. The Joint Commission's intent in incorporating these standards is to ensure that you make competent decisions based on valid, correctly interpreted data. For example, if you wrongly concluded, on the basis of an erroneous data set or an incorrect interpretation, that you needed a major change in your care system, you might diminish your capacity for quality patient care. Similarly, if a lack of knowledge about using valid instrumentation or a lack of awareness about statistical

Table 10.11 Standards Relevant to Staff Knowledge Needs and Evidence of Compliance

Standards	Evidence of Compliance
Expertise in using data (IM.4)	Staff curricula vitae/resumes showing experience Staff with degrees in appropriate field Evidence of relevant staff training reports showing quality of data management
Availability of professional literature (IM.9)	Staff manual/orientation material describing process for accessing professional literature Availability of on-site library Staff education needs surveys Staff interviews Minutes from meetings E-mail showing availability of materials Copies of journal tables of contents regularly supplied to staff

findings produced false positives or false negatives in CQM work, patient care might be affected negatively. You can point out the qualifications of staff who are involved in data-based decisions. If qualified staff members are not available, you should have documentation on your use of consultants. There should also be evidence of advanced training in the use of data for program leaders who make decisions. You reflect this information in employee personnel records, SATP reports/minutes, and course syllabi. Table 10.11 lists ways that you can show compliance with IM.4 and with IM.9, which is addressed next.

Access by Clinical Staff to Relevant Professional Literature (IM.9)

In keeping with the rapid movement of modern care, the Joint Commission wants to ascertain that management and clinical staff can be quickly informed about the latest developments in the field. The knowledge of these developments may come from journals, books, classes, colloquia, or material from computer networks. You can also provide a listing of various interest groups that exchange relevant information on the Internet. We advise that you and your staff use resources available to you. It is understood that this recommendation is in keeping with up-to-date quality care, but there is also a secondary gain; should surveyors interview your staff on this topic, their familiarity with using the literature will be obvious. We suggest that you list your resources. How do staff members go about getting articles? Are you affiliated with a university? Do you have means for underwriting staff education? Do your staff members have access to the Internet? Do your staff members have access to computerized literature searches? Are staff members trained to make use of their resources? We suggest that you explore staff needs in using resources and reflect your findings in needs surveys and in minutes from your staff meetings. We further recommend that you provide training to staff who lack the knowledge to make use of existing resources.

Summary

This chapter has provided an overview of what surveyors look for as they assess your program's use of written and computerized information in the area of patient care and in the area of the organization's monitoring itself and making informed decisions. We have introduced confidentiality, security, integrity, standardization, timeliness, and accuracy in data collection as important topics. We have discussed the need for having a planned method of staff training. We have given suggestions about materials to have on hand as evidence of compliance, and we have detailed what needs to go into various policy memoranda. Finally, we have included an example of the use of aggregated data, along with a discussion of points relevant to using databases.

Surveillance, Prevention, and Control of Infection

Robert G. Hallett
Elizabeth D. Brown
Karen Boies-Hickman

As in all aspects of patient care, the Joint Commission looks to determine the level to which the patient care organization's surveillance, prevention, and control of infection (hereafter referred to as *infection control processes*) are appropriate to usual and anticipated needs of the population served. This chapter provides examples of such processes for specific treatment sites, as well as examples of the integration of these specific activities into a coordinated and comprehensive infection surveillance, prevention, and control mechanism. In this manner, the Joint Commission's approach in assessing the patient care organization's infection control processes is like a clinician's use of systemic theoretical frame-

183

work in conducting an intervention. The goal is to evaluate how the organization's policies, procedures, and practices concerning infection control fit with those of the larger patient care system.

Put simply, the scope and complexity of any infection control process are determined jointly by (a) the acuity level and scope of substance abuse treatment provided within the organization and (b) the generally accepted level of infection known or anticipated within the treatment population treated at the organization's treatment sites. For example, the areas of concern in infection control are quite different for an outpatient clinic and for an acute detoxification unit; processes to address the varying levels of concern should reflect these differences. However, regardless of the acuity level of care provided within an organization, it is imperative that your infection control process be broad enough in scope to address adequately the range of concerns inherent in infection control.

An important consideration to be emphasized is the need to establish and clearly indicate direct linkage between the organization's infection control processes and the larger patient care system. For an inpatient substance abuse detoxification program operating within a large medical care organization, linkage between the unit's infection surveillance procedure and the hospital's infection control committee should be evident within both entities. Alternately, a freestanding methadone clinic's procedures for reporting incidence of infection should be in harmony with guidelines set by local and state public health authorities.

Likewise, the roles played by professional and support staff in the infection control process should reflect a similar linkage application. Responsibilities maintained by specific personnel should be appropriate to skill level and area of expertise. In a large health care system, medical and nursing staffs may and should be responsible for infection control processes identified by both the substance abuse treatment center and their own respective departments. The relationship between these two processes should be clearly evident and free of any conflict. Similar linkage should be readily identified for support staff such as housekeeping and dietary personnel.

Risk Reduction Process (IC.1)

The *MHM* (Joint Commission, 1995) calls for your organization to develop a written plan for infection control that encompasses all patient care and employee health program activities and to show evidence of its implementation. You should be able to show compliance with governing regulations both within the larger organization and with local and state public health agencies. For an acute detoxification program operating within a large medical center, such a process might include a unit-specific infection control plan that references the larger hospital's infection control committee, employee handbook or personnel policies, and patient records. For smaller, freestanding agencies, references should include guidelines from local, state, and/or federal public health authorities. Table 11.1 provides an overview of the applicable specific standards and typical sources of compliance documentation.

Regardless of the size or scope of your organization, the infection control process must address all pertinent areas of patient and staff contact related to possible transmission of infectious disease, as indicated in Table 11.2.

Risk Reduction Mechanisms

Surveillance (IC.2.1)

Surveillance implies an ongoing or continuous process of vigilance against infection routes of transmission. This vigilance is especially pertinent to the substance-abusing patient population, whose behavior is readily associated with highly infectious diseases such as tuberculosis, hepatitis, HIV, and sexually transmitted diseases. However, an effective infection control process should be comprehensive enough to address infection control issues ranging from specific incidents such as an outbreak of gastric disorder associated with food poisoning to an organization-wide review of all infections occurring over a given period of time that identifies trends and calculates overall infection rates. You can easily establish a link from such surveillance to an organizational prevention strategy addressing a particular infection problem or specific patient population.

We recommend that you document routine surveillance activities through periodic chart review and analysis of admission screenings for presence of particular patient maladies associated with high-risk populations. For instance, gather data on persistent coughs potentially as-

Table 11.1   Standards Related to a Risk Reduction Process

Standards	*Evidence of Compliance*
Functioning coordinated processes are in place to reduce risks for endemic and epidemic infection in patients and health care providers (IC.1)	Written plan outlining all activities for infection control and documented reviews of same
Processes include surveillance, prevention, and control mechanisms (IC.1.1)	Job description Clinical privileges Records for training and continuing education Infection control committee (ICC) minutes Scope-of-responsibility statement in bylaws and rules or regulations Interviews with staff, ICC, ICC chair, and administration Document review of policies and procedures of the organization's demographics and definitions of epidemiologically important issues

Table 11.2   Elements to Be Addressed in Infection Control Process

Measures that are scientifically valid, applicable in all settings, and practical to implement

Relationship between employee health activities and the infection surveillance, prevention, and control program

Various methods used to reduce the risk of transmission of infection between or among staff members and between or among patients

Appropriate patient care practices, sterilization, disinfection and antisepsis, and pertinent environmental controls

Educational and consultative roles of the infection control function and personnel

sociated with tuberculosis or abnormal liver function tests linked to hepatitis. You might assess outcomes from such analyses on either a time-limited or a cyclical basis, depending on the structure of the organization's overall infection control plan and the nature of the population served. Table 11.4 outlines the elements that you should consider in addressing the surveillance component of your infection control process.

Table 11.3 Standards Related to Surveillance Mechanisms to Reduce Risks for Endemic and Epidemic Infections

Standards	*Evidence of Compliance*
In patient care and employee health activities, there are mechanisms designed to reduce risks for endemic and epidemic infections (IC.2): Surveillance (IC.2.1) Identification (IC.2.2) Reporting to staff and public health authorities, as required (IC.2.3) Prevention (IC.2.4) Control of infection (IC.2.5)	Policies and procedures in written or electronic format Staff orientation outlines that include infection control content and proof of attendance for each staff member Availability of appropriate laboratory services, either directly or through contract or reference laboratories Infection control committee minutes Scope-of-responsibility statement in bylaws, rules, or regulations Interviews with staff Tours of care units, linen storage areas, dietary and food service areas, and employee health areas Documentation of case-finding and reporting mechanisms both within the organization and to public health agencies Observation of the use of appropriate personal protective equipment and procedures throughout the organization serving an HIV-infected population

Identification (IC.2.2)

Identification refers to the actual means employed to determine the presence of pertinent infection risk factors. Readily known risk factors associated with substance abuse, such as HIV, hepatitis, and TB, are easily documented through literature review and accepted scientific practice. However, factors such as historical data related to environmental concerns, population subgroupings within a community's population, and other similar epidemiological data might require that you document your use of special procedures or practices.

Research projects or studies dealing with new or substantially altered procedures require specific documentation in this area as well as any unusual or sentinel events. Table 11.5 outlines the specific elements to be addressed in the risk identification process.

Table 11.4   Elements to be Addressed by Surveillance Procedures

Problem-oriented or outbreak-response surveillance
  Case-finding methods directed at specific infection problems
Priority-directed, targeted surveillance
  Specific treatment populations, units, or procedures
Total surveillance
  Detects and records all infections in every area of the organization
  Helps to identify potential infection problem areas
  Continuous (large organizations) or periodic (smaller organizations)

Table 11.5   Potential Elements to Be Addressed by Identification Procedures

Literature review for published risk factors

Use of organization-specific historical data

Investigation of clusters of infections above expected levels

Focused studies on procedures with significant potential for infection, particularly when the procedure is new or substantially changed

Comparison of a group of infected patients with an uninfected control group to detect statistically significant risk factors for which control measures can be developed

Reporting (IC.2.3)

As mentioned earlier in this chapter, *reporting* refers to notification both within and outside the organization as appropriate. Units operating as part of a larger health care organization should have clearly established guidelines through the infection control committee or its equivalent that dictate staff roles and expectations related to patient and employee infection reporting. These guidelines should be consistent with personnel policies and patient orientation procedures. It is advisable that cross-references between or among these documents be indicated in the unit's infection control manual. Smaller organizations should consult with the appropriate public health agency in developing their reporting policies and procedures. You should include copies of such documents in your set of infection control policies and procedures.

Table 11.6 Targets of Infection Prevention Policies and Procedures

Patients

Employees

Contractors

Students and volunteers

Family and visitors

Specific environmental issues

Prevention (IC.2.4)

An organization's prevention efforts encompass strategies ranging from immunization to continuing-education activities. Policy and procedure manuals should identify the required prevention strategies for all agency personnel, including students and volunteers. We suggest that you document evidence of specific training well. Table 11.6 identifies the focal areas to be addressed by any infection prevention strategies. You probably should incorporate into your prevention plan measures such as brochures distributed to patients on entering treatment and information handouts made available to family and visitors.

Agencies utilizing large numbers of volunteers and/or students need to be particularly sensitive to orientation efforts concerning infection control and prevention. An orientation plan for either or both, with specific references to infection prevention, registration lists for attendees of infection control and prevention training, immunization documentation from school records, and employee health documentation can be important in delineating your prevention plan.

Control (IC.2.5)

Control mechanisms refers to an organization's response to an identified incident of infection within its treatment population or treatment staff. You should be able to demonstrate clinically and scientifically valid measures to isolate the infection and effectively prevent transmission to other patients, staff, and the larger community.

Supportive documentation, policies and procedures, patient logs, and laboratory and general medical records should indicate compliance with the substance abuse treatment organization's existing infection control plan, as well as that of the larger agency as appropriate. This compliance is especially critical in cases in which a decision may be made to maintain a patient who develops a symptom of an infection, such as diarrhea, while treated on a general ward or within a residential program where potential contact with many individuals is high. The decision-making process leading to such a decision rather than the isolation of the patient should be well documented.

Improvement Measures (IC.3)

Measuring rates of performance improvement in the infection control process is clearly dependent on thorough, ongoing data collection and analysis. Again, in larger organizations, the link between the infection control process of a substance abuse unit and the larger organization should be evident through supportive documentation. Assessments of the data collected and resulting actions taken should indicate a sensitivity to variations in patient risk within the treatment population.

As Table 11.7 demonstrates, infection control committee minutes play a critical role in documenting the decision-making process involved in specific response to data analysis by committee members. You may consider including consultation from sources in and outside the organization in documenting the data analysis portion of these minutes. Comparison of an organization's rates of a particular infection with similar data pertaining to a larger population sample (i.e., Center for Disease Control statistics, state public health agency reports, and findings from other medical centers in the immediate area) will indicate an effort to establish whether such data suggest larger trends to be addressed beyond the organization. Reporting procedures should be clearly established and documented.

Given risks associated with HIV and hepatitis B transmission in the substance abuse treatment population, the need for clear documentation of staff training and continuing-education activities to ensure that they are current and clinically appropriate to the level of staff and treatment population cannot be overstated. Particular attention should be given to education about needle-stick precautions, protective apparel and equipment, and hazardous waste management.

Table 11.7 Standards Related to Improvement in the Risk Reduction Process

Standards	*Evidence of Compliance*
Improvement in the risks for, trends in, and (where appropriate) rates of epidemiologically significant infections is an objective of the infection risk reduction process (IC.3)	A description of the organization's performance-improvement plan, including nosocomial rate improvement activities, such as graphics showing rate improvement
The infection risk reduction process is supported by appropriate management systems to ensure adequate data analysis	Documentation in the budget for infection control support in the following areas: • Equipment • Software • Clerical support Infection control committee or other multidisciplinary minutes A statement of objectives in the infection control program Geographical representation of nosocomial infection risk reduction (NIRR) achieved

PART 3

Pulling It Together

12

The Human Side of Preparing for the Accreditation Visit

Sigmund Hough
Elizabeth D. Brown

Preparing for an accreditation visit can be a challenging experience, characterized at times by a sense of despair and at other times by a sense of satisfaction for having completed another requirement. Every program manager knows that the Joint Commission may grant full or conditional accreditation or may decide to deny accreditation. Conditional accreditation is granted to organizations that are not substantially in compliance with standards but are considered to be capable of timely resolution of existing problems. The Joint Commission denies accreditation to organizations with severe performance problems or widespread noncompliance with the standards.

The intent of this book is to help you to gain full accreditation. In addition to the technical issues of meeting the standards, the organizational processes needed to meet the demands of Joint Commission requirements must be in tune with the human realities of relationship, true performance capabilities, and high staff morale. Thus we end this book with some tips to assist you and your staff with a practical approach to preparing for the accreditation visit and an examination of the human side of preparing a program for accreditation. Even when you do well during a survey, you and others will feel the stress of being judged. Therefore, we also recommend ways to minimize the stress that the accreditation process often generates.

Part of our reasoning for including practical advice comes from our belief that it is important to recognize that not all programs can be all things for all people. When we extend the topic of patient care to substance abuse, the various activities usually take on a more complex character, for substance abuse care requires a truly systemic approach both within the individual patient and within the socioecological world that he or she inhabits. This very complexity becomes vexing, particularly in those programs that have limited resources. In these instances, we advise clinicians to think about what is workable and needed for patient care rather than trying to second-guess what a surveyor will seek. We do not mean to imply that you should ignore Joint Commission criteria and scoring guidelines; rather, you should read them with attention to what works within the clinical program. It is understood that you should continue to ensure that the care of patients is as compatible with Joint Commission requirements as possible and that all recording is adequate. For example, after reading this book, readers should be well aware of the need to place great emphasis on assessments that are both interdisciplinary and integrated. However, at times program personnel may deem some component to be unworkable within their program's structure. Under these circumstances, you should put the rationale for that decision into writing, explore alternate mechanisms for delivering the component, and gather data on the effects of not having the component. The tenor of these statements is to encourage you not to fall into a state of paralysis when you find shortcomings but rather to explore proactively the best fit between your program and the criteria with which surveyors will examine it.

Getting Prepared

First, we urge you to be *organized*. You and your staff will feel less anxiety about the upcoming visit if you feel that you are well prepared. We strongly recommend that you have in place all key elements that will catch the interest of the surveyors. Further, you should try to accomplish this task at least 12 months before the survey visit so that you can show a good track record. Changes will occur during the 12-month period. Your documentation should give evidence of what existed before the change, how the decision-making process behind the change went, and the current method of operating.

We have found it useful to have three-ring binders for organizing documentation. As you look back through this book and read the *MCM*'s scoring guidelines, you can decide on which materials you will be putting in the binders. For example, your memoranda, letters of agreement, and staffing contracts may be in one place. Each person has his or her own system of organization; you may want to have personnel-related materials in another place and CQM information in still a third place. What matters is that you can retrieve materials quickly and efficiently. We use section separators and tabs to help to get to the material efficiently. We have also found it helpful to have templates naming types of evidence on the abscissa and various standards on the ordinate. With this approach, we check off the evidence that we have for two purposes. First, this method helps us to ensure that we have enough on a given topic. Second, it reminds us to retrieve information that we might have forgotten. If your adopt this strategy, you may want to provide the surveyor with a copy of the template if you believe that it will assist him or her. We also find it useful to enlist our staff's help in filling out the templates. Some material that has seemed sufficient to us has not appeared adequate to some of our staff. When we encounter such an outcome, we re-examine the material that originally we thought useful. Having the assistance of staff members in this exercise has also brought to light some useful evidence that we might otherwise have forgotten.

Early steps toward organizing for the visit also may help your staff to feel more involved and empowered. One of the authors of this chapter recently reviewed a notice from a private hospital stating, "As you know, the Joint Commission survey is upon us and we are required to meet certain standards related to our respective roles. . . . I have enclosed the most recent updated policy outlining each of our responsibilities." This notice was the first Joint Commission memorandum sent that year. Such communication represents an example of what we call a "last-minute problem-focused solution"—in other words, "a quick fix." The message, albeit unintended, that the employee received was "Here is a task that must be done for these outsiders who are important, so you had better shape up or else."

As part of your early organization work, we recommend that you try to look at your program through a surveyor's eyes. For example, as we encouraged you to do in Chapter 8, walk through your program areas trying to think as a stranger would. Do the areas look clean and welcoming? Are there frayed rugs or tiles on which someone might trip? Is there sufficient light? Do staff offices allow for privacy of patient care? We have included a checklist in Appendix E that may help you as you make your tours.

We strongly recommend that you work with your staff on *rehearsing* interactions with the survey visitors. Staff should be able to anticipate questions that may be asked. One very worthwhile strategy involves assigning different staff members to the role of a surveyor in these mock visits. This move involves staff members more and helps them to see the program as a surveyor will.

We suggest that you promote *cohesion* both among the members of your team and with the parent organization. You can encourage staff members to participate in facility-wide committees and to report developments to the team. This participation should foster camaraderie among staff members and break down barriers between departments and services.

You always should remember that laughter is usually indicative of good mental health (Fry & Salameh, 1987). Good *humor* is a tremendous stress reliever and a healthy component in communication. When the survey is around the corner, try to diminish some of the performance anxiety by introducing levity. At one medical center, the assistant chief of the psychiatry service attended a workshop on the value of fun in the workplace. He then initiated E-mail for various contests such as completing limericks.

The humor intervention was infectious, and other staff members soon got engaged in it. Staff initiated a newsletter with editorial columns written by Sir Veyor and others. One of the department heads did an amusing E-mail entry in SOAP note format (a treatment note addressing patient's Subjective presentations, clinician's Objective observations, clinician's Assessment, and clinician's Plan for treatment).

In short, there was often something humorous to elevate morale throughout the month or two prior to the survey. One of the "contests" had to do with predicting the survey date, with the winner treated to a cup of specialty coffee. None of these efforts consumed much time (for instance, 5 to 10 minutes for a limerick verse). At the end of the week before the site visit, mental health leaders had a pep "congratulations" rally for all mental health staff. Guest appearances (in costume) were made by those who had contributed to the newsletter. Ms. Manners (appropriately garbed in gloves and a veiled hat) gently reminded staff of how to be courteous to each other, to clients, and to visitors. Following the visit and before the results were obtained, the medical center gave a show of appreciation to staff by hosting a picnic, complete with dunking booths for some of the administrative heads and other staff. When the news was finally in, everyone got together to hear the results. They had obtained a perfect score in both the survey and staff morale!

Conflict and disagreement are normal parts of team functioning and development. What is crucial is the manner in which you handle them. Despite differences of opinion, you and your team must still meet objectives. You should encourage productive disagreement, respect for different opinions, and adherence to the final decision. With such an approach, your staff members can learn from each other and help your program in its improvement efforts. To this end, a humanistic strategic plan will enhance your survey preparation. If growth is to come from conflict, it has to occur in the company of good communication (Whitbourne & Weinstock, 1979, pp. 158-161). We shall say more on this topic later.

You need to think about your *leadership* in the program. To be effective as a leader, you need the respect of your staff. We suggest that you consider being a role model for the types of behavior that you want to find in your staff. Much like a family, organizations need authoritative figures who are respected and who can provide role modeling. In addition, as noted by Lundberg (1982), a successful leader is an individual who

- Knows where he or she is going
- Knows how to get there
- Has courage and persistence
- Can be believed
- Can be trusted not to "sell out" a cause for personal advantage
- Makes the mission seem important, exciting, and possible to accomplish
- Makes each person's role in the mission seem important
- Makes each member feel capable of performing his or her role

Communication is another key element of your effective preparation. As survey readiness intensifies, tempers may become short. As a leader, you will want to keep up a steady infusion of morale. In doing so, it is essential to know your team. You are the best suited to know which strategies will boost morale and which will generate frustration and resentment. We advise that you limit clichés and slogans such as "zero deficiencies or bust" and "quality is number one." These imply that workers could do better if only they tried harder. Such an approach may offend those already working above capacity and engender a feeling of not being appreciated. Instead, we recommend that you serve as a role model for effective, positive, and open communication. We strongly suggest that you keep your team apprised of relevant information and that you seek feedback from all staff. Furthermore, when delegating responsibilities, you should explain the rationale behind the required change or request for conformity. Instead of stating, "You now have to use these words when writing progress notes," you can explain that you need standardized terminology to compare care provided by your program with care provided at other treatment settings. Your staff also might be interested in knowing that standardization of terminology may be important from a reimbursement perspective.

Another strategy is to make use of *consultants*. Consultants can be external or internal. Each type of consultant has positive and negative characteristics (Brown, 1980). External consultants with expert knowledge can provide insight and new ideas, but they will need time to know the organization and to gain the trust of employees. Internal consultants are already employed by the facility and have additional knowledge in a needed area. On the negative side, internal consultants may be too close to problems and may have lessened credibility with some staff members.

A financial incentive to using internal consultants is that there is no fee for their contribution.

Continuous quality management (CQM) is no longer an ideal in health and psychiatric care. It is an indicator of an organization's potential for survival. A comprehensive approach to the assessment and treatment of substance-abusing patients includes ongoing evaluations of effectiveness and improvements of care. This approach must include the staff as an integral part of the performance of the system and its processes. Effective CQM requires that staff understand what to expect and participate in improvement efforts.

Managing Stress

At some point in your preparation process, you will probably find yourself thinking, "This sounds like a great deal of work. Can it all come together in time?" As you prepare for survey, the usual amount of stress experienced on the job will no doubt intensify. A situation that demands change and adaptation causes stress by burdening the mental and physical systems of the human body.

The literature informs us that there is good stress, which gears you up and into productive action (Weiss, 1980). We also know that there is bad stress that debilitates and immobilizes you to the point of being unable to perform at your best. Most surveyors can tune quickly into the emotional climate of the workplace. Thus it is to your advantage to motivate your staff to be productive and to reduce as much as possible tensions that may add to bad stress. We recommend several strategies that you may consider. The first bit of advice involves clear communication with your staff so that they will know what to expect. As your staff members' expectations become clearer, they should feel more in control and less stressed.

Stress can be generated by fear (loss of job), lack of predictability, and lack of control. Such stress is more likely to occur if you have not planned far in advance for the survey visit. In such situations, employees are left wondering why there was inadequate preplanning and preparation. Employees who have not been asked to assist in adequate preparations also can feel undervalued, especially if they are given the message that they are simply to follow instructions. There is something paradoxical here. You may be thinking of the complaints that you often hear when you ask your staff to take on new responsibilities. People complain about not having enough time, and you may hear similar complaints when you ask staff to put effort into site visit preparation activities. But fundamentally, most staff members want to feel respected and valued for their contributions to the organization. Without that connection, there is little hope that everyone will consistently put in the effort to comply, much less to improve compliance to standards.

Another example of bad stress occurs when an organization attempts to intimidate employees with threats of losing their jobs or being demoted. These actions are short-sighted and dysfunctional in the long run. Even if the organization achieves a successful survey, team-building efforts have been destroyed. There will be decreased motivation and negative energy in the work arena. In addition, these actions foster resentment toward continued compliance and quality enhancement.

We encourage you to practice some basic principles of stress management. You may find it appropriate to provide a workshop for your staff members so that they, too, can know what to do to reduce stress (see Benson, 1976; LeShan, 1974). These principles include the following:

- Exercise.
- Maintain healthy eating habits.
- Promote functional sleep patterns.
- Cultivate outside interests.
- Promote positive and productive communication.
- Seek continuing education to increase knowledge, competency, and self-esteem.
- Establish a calm and relaxing period during the day.
- Make time to be with peers who can offer support, ideas, feedback, and a professional perspective for emotional balance.
- Use meditation, visual imagery, and deep-relaxation techniques.
- Use time management techniques.
- Set realistic short-term objectives that lead to long-term goals.

Other strategies for stress reduction involve increasing self-awareness and identifying specific solutions to difficult problems.

To promote *self-awareness*, you need to know yourself and use what has worked best for you in the past. You also need to identify what has not worked so that you can avoid those approaches. For example, if you know that you have a tendency to procrastinate, you will have to break down Joint Commission standards into steps with target dates and develop a time schedule. Give yourself some rewards as you meet your self-imposed requirements. These rewards need not be big things. For example, when you finish your requirement for the day, you might want to turn on a radio station that you particularly like. You also may want to enlist the help of others (e.g., a co-worker or other members of a quality assurance committee on which you serve) to keep you on track. If your strength lies in organizational skills, identify specific solutions, follow the principles of stress management (Woolfolk & Lehrer, 1984), and use relaxation dynamics techniques (Smith, 1985) for self-relaxation.

In *identifying specific solutions* to difficult problems, focus on what the standard requires and how to meet it rather than allowing yourself to get caught in the philosophy of how the standard was written. One of the authors once participated as a member of a clinical team that wasted several weeks debating over whether a standard was fair and how they would change things if only they had a chance. Eventually, they moved from debating to doing, from generating problems to ensuring compliance, and from feeling frustrated to feeling successful and effective.

Interacting With Surveyors

Whether you call them surveyors, accreditation visitors, or site visitors, the image that staff form of the accreditation team is one of power. The surveyors have what you want—their seal of approval. One way to lessen evaluation anxiety is to view the accreditation visit as a process of checks and balances for the organization to succeed. In fact, Joint Commission surveyors typically see themselves in dual roles. The first role, that of an evaluator, is the one that program staff expect and the one that creates stress. However, there is a second role—that of an educator. You should make sure that your staff members know of this benign side of the evaluative process so that they can capitalize on its positive aspects rather than seeing the accreditation team members as antagonists. For example, one of the writers for this chapter has had experience in one disastrous survey visit. The quality assurance officer had assessed the substance abuse treatment program's preparations as well done.

Accordingly, the staff members were prepared for a laudatory response from the surveyor. However, as it turned out, the preparations were far less than adequate. There was insufficient attention to defining memoranda, to issues related to staff credentialing, and to other important issues. Rather than using the surveyor as a consultant to know how to correct matters, two program leaders consistently challenged the surveyor and argued against her comments and concerns. Needless to say, the program was subjected to a later focused survey.

Instead, consider the following exchange:

> **Surveyor:**   There seems to be too long a period in getting assessment data in this section of your outpatient program.
>
> **Program Leader:**   That is a problem. We have tried [give examples] and have been stymied each time. This [give an example] is what we're trying right now. Have you found this problem in other programs like ours? Do you have any suggestions for correction?

You should think about how to make the surveyor comfortable. Take steps for reserving a readily identifiable parking place. Does he or she want a cup of coffee or a soft drink? Does he or she need time for a smoking break? How does he or she want the day scheduled? Plan for an organized but comfortable visit with the surveyor. If he or she is planning to meet with groups of staff, is it possible to have refreshments nearby to promote a more relaxed atmosphere? If you have a horticulture program, can you get flowers or plants brought to sites where staff will meet?

We recommend that you use backup measures to prevent problems that may occur. One of these steps might be to have staff on hand who do not work directly with your patients. For instance, we have had a pharmacist sit in on a surveyor's interview with inpatient staff. His information about certain medications being used answered a surveyor's concerns in a way that the treating physician's had not. Another important bit of advice is to have a staff member running interference to detect any problems before the surveyor gets to any particular site. For example, while the surveyor was meeting with inpatient staff, someone walked ahead to the surveyor's next destination at the outpatient program. As it turned out, the air conditioner in the program's meeting room chose, on that 98° day, to malfunction. Another meeting room was arranged before the surveyor arrived at the program.

Maintenance

After the surveyors have left your facility, there is a tendency to say, "We got through that one. Now let's get back to business as usual." In doing so, you are at risk for a repeated cycle of frenzied preparation, survey, and relaxation of standards. A more effective strategy rests on maintaining the structure now in place. Furthermore, in a change from past practice, the Joint Commission now makes unannounced surveys on a random basis. This new practice should motivate all of us to keep our programs survey-ready. We recommend that you continue to discuss accreditation during staff meetings and in orienting new staff members. This framework will establish clear expectations and standards of work performance. You should include adherence to Joint Commission standards in employees' annual performance evaluations.

Finally, we urge you to remember the social side of preparation. For example, you might consider working lunches to improve quality of care and to maintain continuous survey preparedness. Team members bring lunch to brainstorm solutions by listening, educating, and strategizing. Your goal is to create an environment where people feel safe making suggestions. Most important, because food is a basic human need and people often work through their lunch hour anyway, you stand a good chance of involving the entire team.

In closing, some view *change* as the most frightening word in the English language. Instead, we think that stagnation is the most frightening decision that one could ever make. With change comes opportunity, with opportunity comes hope, with hope comes satisfaction. In the months and years ahead, incorporate these fundamentals of accreditation:

J   =   *Join*—Everyone participates throughout the process.
C   =   *Clarity and Communication*—Help employees to feel control and empowerment by communicating openly and well about what is needed.
A   =   *Attitude*—Reality based and positive; focus more on what you can accomplish instead of why you cannot.
H   =   *Humor*—A little humor goes a long way during a long day.
O   =   *Organized*—Organizational skills and streamlined systems are the foundations for building systems of quality care.

Appendix A

Form Giving Consent
to Act as a Participant in a
Research Study (Intervention)

TITLE: Brief Intervention and Stage of Change in Primary Care

INVESTIGATOR: _____

COINVESTIGATOR: _____

SOURCE OF SUPPORT: National Institutes of Health

PURPOSE: The purpose of this study is to learn more about the alcohol use of primary health care patients, as well as the effectiveness of advice and counseling of medical doctors or nurses in effecting change in alcohol consumption.

DESCRIPTION: I understand that I may be asked to participate in from one to three counseling sessions designed to learn more about how patients do when they are encouraged to change their alcohol use through the advice and counseling of medical doctors or nurses. I may be asked to participate because I use alcohol and I have a regular doctor at this Blue Cross and Blue Shield Health Center. These sessions would be held at the clinic site and would include breath alcohol tests. Each session would take at least 15 minutes but no longer than 1 hour.

In addition, I will be contacted by telephone in 1 month, in 3 months, and in 9 months and asked questions about how I am doing in terms of my health and health habits. These telephone conversations will take approximately 20 minutes. I will be asked to return to the clinic after 6 months and 1 year for further evaluations, blood pressure checks, and blood tests. These visits will take about 1 hour. There will be approximately 100 patients asked to participate in this study (50 men and 50 women).

At the end of this consent form, I will be asked to supply the names of two family members or friends and give permission for them to be contacted and asked questions about how things are going for me. In addition, I will be asked to provide the name of one individual who may be contacted, if necessary, to determine my whereabouts for reassessment. The questions asked of my family and friends will be similar to those asked of me. I also understand that only those people whose names I have given will be contacted and that at no time, and under no circumstances, will any information about me be shared with a collateral, and vice versa.

RISKS AND BENEFITS: There will be minimal risks to me. I understand that there is a small risk of pain, bleeding, and bruising at the site if blood is taken. I may benefit by learning more about how the use of alcohol affects my health and

207

my lifestyle. In addition, I may receive help in trying to change my alcohol use if I decide to do so.

COSTS AND PAYMENTS: There will be no cost to me as a result of the study. I will be paid $25 for completing each in-person evaluation and $10 for each phone evaluation I complete. I understand that each family member or friend contacted by phone will be paid $10 for each contact.

I also understand that I would not be paid for attending counseling sessions. Payment is made for evaluation sessions only.

Appendix B

Outline of Intake Screening Note for
Specialized Outpatient Spouse-Involved SATP

Demographic description: (include age, race/ethnicity, education, employment, years married or living together, prior marriages for both partners)

Children (at home and away) are: (names, ages, and special concerns)

Referral source and reason why couple is seeking treatment now:

Interview behavior:

Psychoactive substance use disorders:
(brief statement about current and history for both partners)

Relationship stability: (current, prior, planned separations)

Domestic violence: (current and history for both partners)

Suicidal or homicidal thoughts and behavior:
(current and history for both partners)

Alcohol-related or other crises or major stressors:

DSM diagnostic impression and plan:

Appendix C

Diagnostic Summary

Mr. Larry Duke is a 48-year-old married, marginally self-employed, non-service-connected United States Marine Corps combat veteran who received a Purple Heart for his service in Vietnam. He is the oldest of three brothers, one of whom has a history of substance abuse and is HIV-positive. He married in 1971, divorced in 1976, and remarried his first wife, Marge, in 1980. They have two sons, ages 12 and 15. Their younger son is diagnosed with ADHD and receives counseling and medication. The couple presented to our couples therapy outpatient clinic after responding to a newspaper ad and requested help for relationship and family problems engendered by Mr. Duke's periodic binge drinking and excessive gambling.

Mr. Duke's current problems appear to have evolved from a dysfunctional and physically abusive family environment, extensive exposure to combat, and controlling and narcissistic personality features that have prevented him from seeking and accepting professional help until now. He has struggled with a number of addictive and impulse control disorders, including alcoholism, abuse of prescription and street drugs, nicotine addiction, and pathological gambling. Although he recently quit smoking because he has emphysema, his recent abuse of alcohol and cocaine, and significant financial losses incurred by gambling, have caused enormous marital and family problems. Because he refused recommendations to enter an inpatient addiction rehabilitation center, the primary goals of his outpatient treatment are to stabilize his drinking and drug use behaviors, to decrease gambling behavior, and to work on family problems using a spouse-involved behavioral therapy approach. Once abstinence is achieved and progress is made in other areas, Mr. Duke will be referred for further evaluation and treatment of post-traumatic stress disorder.

DSM-IV DIAGNOSES

I.	Alcohol Dependence	303.90
	Cocaine Abuse	305.60
	Cannabis Abuse	305.20
	PTSD, Chronic	309.81
	Pathological Gambling	312.31
	Partner Relational Problem	V61.1
	Parent-Child Relational Problem	V61.20
II.	Rule-out Antisocial Personality Disorder	
	Rule-out Narcissistic Personality Disorder	
III.	Emphysema	
IV.	Stressors: Marital and family discord, financial debt, job difficulties	
V.	GAF (Current)	65

PROBLEM LIST

A. Problems to Be Addressed

1. *Psychoactive Substance Use Disorders:* Manifested by periodic binge drinking, use of cocaine and marijuana

2. *PTSD:* Manifested by avoidance of trauma stimuli and emotional numbing, intrusive memories associated with combat and loss, irritability and angry outbursts, hypervigilance and anxiety, sleep problems, and difficulty interacting with authority figures. Treatment in this clinic will focus on educating patient and spouse about symptoms of the disorder (psychoeducational approach).

3. *Pathological Gambling:* Manifested by persistent purchase of lottery tickets and playing video poker beyond financial means, "chasing" to recoup losses, failed attempts to cut down or stop gambling, and severe financial losses.

4. *Marital Discord:* Manifested by actual and recurrent threat of separation; distrust, alienation, and poor communication.

5. *Parenting Problems:* Manifested by parental inconsistency and difficulty managing ADHD child.

B. Problems Identified but Not Treated and Reason Why

1. *Emphysema:* Patient is currently under the care of his private physicians outside the VA system.

2. *PTSD:* Patient will be referred to specialty clinics for further evaluation and treatment of trauma issues, and assistance with applying for veterans benefits/disability.

Appendix D

Sample of Items That Could Be Included
in an SATP Education Component Checklist

Education Component	Date Patient Exposed (If Relevant)	Date Patient's Family Exposed (If Relevant)
Medical consequences of alcohol and other drug use		
Use of self-help organizations		
Relapse prevention		
Role of the family in recovery		
Physical interactions among alcohol and other drugs		
Effects of alcohol on psychotropic medication		

Appendix E

Rounds Checklist

UNIT _____   DATE _____

PSYCHIATRIST _____ (PRESENT/ABSENT)

HEAD NURSE _____ (PRESENT/ABSENT)

Patient Rooms

(Y) (N)   Bulletin board with personal items posted
(Y) (N)   Toiletries in night stand
(Y) (N)   Matched bedspreads
(Y) (N)   Draperies
(Y) (N)   Laundry stored appropriately
(Y) (N)   Patient identification on each bed
(Y) (N)   Plants
(Y) (N)   Patient closets/lockers in working order
(Y) (N)   Overall cleanliness
(Y) (N)   Framed art present
(Y) (N)   Other

Patient Bathrooms

(Y) (N)   Odor
(Y) (N)   Shower utilized and functional
(Y) (N)   Clean
(Y) (N)   Toilets and seats in good repair
(Y) (N)   Other

Dayroom

(Y) (N)   Clean
(Y) (N)   Functioning television
(Y) (N)   Current magazines
(Y) (N)   Fully utilized for patient activities
(Y) (N)   Framed art present
(Y) (N)   Evidence of staff and patient activities
(Y) (N)   Furniture matches and is in good repair
(Y) (N)   Plants present
(Y) (N)   Other

Corridor

(Y)   (N)   Orientation board present and up to date
(Y)   (N)   30-day activity calendar posted, up to date, complete, legible
(Y)   (N)   Activities noted for days/evenings/weekends
(Y)   (N)   Lighting is appropriate
(Y)   (N)   Walls need repair/touch-up painting
(Y)   (N)   Framed art present
(Y)   (N)   Postings are current, well organized, and legible
(Y)   (N)   Decorations reflect upcoming holiday
(Y)   (N)   Clean
(Y)   (N)   Odor
(Y)   (N)   Clutter in corridor
(Y)   (N)   Other

Patient Dining Room

(Y)   (N)   Clean
(Y)   (N)   Mops/buckets out of view
(Y)   (N)   Framed art present
(Y)   (N)   Other

Other Observations

(+)   (-)   Team interaction
(+)   (-)   Staff appearance/appropriateness
(Y)   (N)   ID badges worn by staff
(Y)   (N)   Staff congregates in nursing station
(Y)   (N)   Supply closet neat and well organized
(Y)   (N)   Seclusion rooms used appropriately
(Y)   (N)   Patient/family visiting room clean, matching furniture,
            framed artwork

References

American Psychiatric Association. (1994). *Diagnostic and statistical manual of mental disorders* (4th ed.). Washington, DC: Author.

Beck, A. T., & Beamesderfer, A. (1974). Assessment of depression: The Beck Depression Inventory. In P. Pichot (Ed.), *Psychological measurements in psychopharmacology* (pp. 151-169). Basel, Switzerland: Karger.

Bender, L. (1938). *A Visual Motor Gestalt Test and its clinical use* (American Orthopsychiatric Association Research Monograph No. 3). New York: American Orthopsychiatric Association.

Benson, H. (1976). *The relaxation response.* New York: Avon.

Brown, E. D. (1980). Effective training of program evaluators: A mixture of art and science. *New Directions for Program Evaluation, 8,* 79-87.

Butcher, J. N., Dahlstrom, W. G., Graham, J. R., Tellegen, A., & Kaemmer, B. (1989). *Minnesota Multiphasic Personality Inventory-2 (MMPI-2): Manual for administration and scoring.* Minneapolis: University of Minnesota Press.

Doak, C. C., Doak, L. G., & Root, J. H. (1985). *Teaching patients with low literacy skills.* Philadelphia: J. B. Lippincott.

Fry, W. F., Jr., & Salameh, W. A. (Eds.). (1987). *Handbook of humor and psychotherapy: Advances in the clinical use of humor.* Sarasota, FL: Professional Resource Exchange.

Graham, F. K., & Kendall, B. S. (1960). Memory-for-Designs Test: Revised general manual. *Perceptual and Motor Skills, 11*(Monograph Suppl. No. 2), 147-188.

Institute of Medicine. (1990). *Broadening the base of treatment for alcohol problems.* Washington, DC: National Academy Press.

Joint Commission on Accreditation of Healthcare Organizations. (1993, June). *Accreditation manual for pathology and clinical laboratory services (LSM).* Oakbrook Terrace, IL: Author.

Joint Commission on Accreditation of Healthcare Organizations. (1995). *The 1995 accreditation manual for mental health, chemical dependency, and mental retardation/developmental disabilities services (MHM)* (2 vols.). Oakbrook Terrace, IL: Author.

LeShan, L. (1974) *How to meditate*. Boston: Little, Brown.

Lundberg, L. B. (1982). What is leadership? *Journal of Nursing Administration, 12*, 32-33.

Maisto, S. A., McKay, J. R., & O'Farrell, T. J. (1995). Relapse precipitants and behavioral marital therapy. *Addictive Behaviors, 20*, 383-393.

McLellan, A. T., Luborsky, L., Cacciola, J., Griffith, J., Evans, F., Barr, H. L., & O'Brien, C. P. (1985). New data from the Addiction Severity Index: Reliability and validity in three centers. *Journal of Nervous and Mental Disease, 173*, 412-423.

Miller, W. R., & Rollnick, S. (1991). *Motivational interviewing: Preparing people to change addictive behaviors*. New York: Guilford.

Millon, T. (1994). *Millon Clinical Multiaxial Inventory III: Manual for the MCMI-III*. Minneapolis: National Computer Systems.

Moos, R. H. (1988). *Community-Oriented Programs Environment Scale manual* (2nd ed.). Palo Alto, CA: Consulting Psychologists Press.

Moos, R. H. (1989). *Ward Atmosphere Scale manual* (2nd ed.). Palo Alto, CA: Consulting Psychologists Press.

O'Farrell, T. J. (1993). A behavioral marital therapy couples group program for alcoholics and their spouses. In T. J. O'Farrell (Ed.), *Treating alcohol problems: Marital and family interventions* (pp. 170-209). New York: Guilford.

O'Farrell, T. J., & Langenbucher, J. (1988). Time-line drinking behavior interview. In M. Hersen & A. Bellack (Eds.), *Dictionary of behavioral assessment techniques* (pp. 477-479). New York: Pergamon.

Peterson, K. A., Swindle, R. W., Phibbs, C. S., Recine, B., & Moos, R. H. (1994). Determinants of readmission following inpatient substance abuse treatment: A national study of VA programs. *Medical Care, 32*, 535-550.

Quay, H. C. (1977). The three faces of evaluation: What can be expected to work. *Criminal Justice and Behavior, 44*, 341-354.

Reitan, R. M., & Wolfson, D. (1985). *The Halstead-Reitan Neuropsychological Test Battery*. Tucson, AZ: Neuropsychology Press.

Selzer, M. L. (1979). The Michigan Alcoholism Screening Test: The quest for a new diagnostic instrument. *American Journal of Psychiatry, 127*, 1653-1658.

Shipley, W. C. (1940). A self-administered scale for measuring intellectual impairment and deterioration. *Journal of Psychology, 9*, 371-377.

Smith, J. C. (1985). *Relaxation dynamics: A cognitive-behavioral approach to relaxation*. Champaign, IL: Research Press.

Sobell, L. C., & Sobell, M. B. (1996). Timeline follow-back: A calendar program for assessing alcohol and drug use. Toronto: Addiction Research Foundation.

Spielberger, C. D., Gorsuch, R. L., & Lushene, R. E. (1970). *Test manual for the State-Trait Anxiety Inventory*. Palo Alto, CA: Consulting Psychologists Press.

Wanberg, K. W., & Horn, J. L. (1983). Assessment of alcohol use with multidimensional concepts and measures. *American Psychologist, 38*, 1055-1070.

Wechsler, D. (1981). *Wechsler Adult Intelligence Scale-Revised*. New York: Psychological Corporation.

Wechsler, D. (1987). *Wechsler Memory Scale-Revised.* New York: Psychological Corporation.

Weedman, R. D. (1992). *Patient records in addiction treatment: Documenting the quality of care.* Oakbrook Terrace, IL: Joint Commission on Accreditation of Healthcare Organizations.

Weiss, W. H. (1980). *Supervisor's standard reference handbook.* Englewood Cliffs, NJ: Prentice Hall.

Whitbourne, S. K., & Weinstock, C. S. (1979). *Adult development: The differentiation of experience.* New York: Holt, Rinehart & Winston.

Woolfolk, R. L., & Lehrer, P. M. (Eds.). (1984). *Principles and practice of stress management.* New York: Guilford.

Index

ASAM, 25
Assessment of:
  Abuse or neglect, 43-45, 50.
    See also PE.1.15, PE.1.18
  Chemical dependency, 46-50.
    See also PE.1.18
  Children and adolescents, 45-46.
    See also PE.1.16
  Competence, 151-153, 154-156.
    See also HR.3, HR.5
  CQM, 99-102
  Determination of additional, 43.
    See also PE.1.13
  Emotional and behavioral, 34-37.
    See also PE.1.5
  Environment, 132-140. *See also* EC.1
    through EC.3
  Functional status, 33-34. *See also*
    PE.1.4 and PE.1.4.1
  Legal, 41. *See also* PE.1.8
  Memory, 35
  Needs, 132-140, 164. *See also* EC.1
    through EC.3, IM.1
  Nutritional status, 33, 68. *See also*
    PE.1, TX.4
  Patients, 29-54. *See also* PE.1 through
    PE.4
  Physical health, 41-42, 49. *See also*
    PE.1
  Psychiatric, 35-36
  Psychosocial, 37-43. *See also* PE.1
  Risk, 32-33. *See also* PE.1

Screening and Initial, 14-16, 30-31,
    34, 44-45, 209. *See also* CC.1
    and CC.2, or PE.1
  Spiritual orientation, 49-50.
    See also PE.1.18
  Staff needs, 121-123. *See also* LD.2
  Staff rights, 153-154
  Timing of, 111
  Vocational/educational, 40-41.
    See also PE.1.7

Beck et al., 36
Bender, L., 36
Benson, H., 201-203. *See also* LeShan, L.,
    Smith, J. C., Stress, management of,
    Weiss, W. H, Woolfolk, R. L.
Brown, E. D., 200-201
Butcher, J. N., 36

Case formulation, 51-52. *See also* PE.2,
    Diagnostic summary
CC.1, 14-16. *See also* Assessment,
    screening and initial
CC.2, 14-16. *See also* Assessment,
    screening and initial
CC.3, 16-17. *See also* Patient, care
    options
  CC.3.1 through CC.3.5, 18.
    See also Patient, informed
    decision making
CC.4, 19. *See also* Continuum of care
CC.5, 19. *See also* Continuum of care

About the Editors

Karen Boies-Hickman, PhD, was Deputy Associate Chief for Addictive Disorders in the Mental Health Strategic Health Group, Veterans Health Administration, Department of Veterans Affairs. In this position, she supported the associate chief in the development and management of substance abuse treatment services provided to veterans in nearly 160 VA medical facilities. Prior to her appointment, she held program development and monitoring positions in VA offices responsible for national programs of vocational rehabilitation for veterans with compensable disabilities and services for geriatric and extended-care patients. For over 10 years, she worked at a psychiatric facility for the chronically mentally ill, where she directed a behavior therapy unit and the hospital's quality assurance program. She has been a part-time surveyor for the Joint Commission on Accreditation of Health Care Organizations and is licensed for independent practice of psychology in the state of Virginia.

Elizabeth D. Brown, PhD, is Assistant Clinical Professor of Psychology in the Department of Psychiatry at the Harvard Medical School. She formerly was Assistant Professor in the Clinical/Community Psychology Program and in the Applied Development Program at the University of Maryland in College Park. She currently is Chief of the Psychology Service at the Veterans Affairs Medical Center in Brockton, West Roxbury, and Worcester, Massachusetts. She has served on a number of national committees for the Department of Veterans Affairs, including chairing the Special Projects on Substance Abuse Group. She also served as a delegate of Donna Shalala, Secretary of Health and Human Services to the 1995 White House Conference on Aging. She has successfully writ-ten several clinical grants for substance programming and has provided the initial program development for each of these projects. She also established the outpatient substance abuse program at the Fort Howard, Maryland, Department of Veterans Affairs Medical Center. She earned her doctorate in clinical psychology at the Florida State University.

Stephen A. Maisto, PhD, is Professor of Psychology at Syracuse University. He previously had academic appointments as Associate Professor of Psychology in the Department of Psychiatry and Human Behavior at Brown University; as Associate Professor in the Department of Psychiatry, University of Pittsburgh Medical School; and as Assistant Professor in the Department of Psychology at Vanderbilt University. He has provided clinical services on public and private alcohol treatment settings for over 20 years. He is on the editorial board of two journals and has published four books, in addition to the present one, in the substance abuse area. He has many research publications and currently is working on research funded by the National Institutes of Health on alcohol and drug treat-ment process and outcome. He received his doctoral degree in experi-mental psychology at the University of Wisconsin at Milwaukee and completed a postdoctoral specialization in clinical psychology at Vander-bilt University.

Timothy F. O'Farrell, PhD, is Associate Professor of Psychology in the Department of Psychiatry at Harvard Medical School, where he directs the Harvard Families and Addiction Program and the Harvard Counsel-ing for Alcoholics' Marriages (CALM) Project. He is also Associate Chief of the Psychology Service at the Veterans Affairs Medical Center in Brockton and West Roxbury, Massachusetts. He has published more than 130 articles, chapters, and papers, primarily on marital and family therapy in alcoholism treatment and various aspects of alcoholics' family relationships. His books include *Alcohol and Sexuality* (1983) and *Treat-ing Alcohol Problems: Marital and Family Interventions* (1993). He is a Fellow of Division 12 (Clinical Psychology) of the American Psychologi-cal Association and Chair of the Special Interest Group on Addictive Behaviors of the Association for the Advancement of Behavior Therapy. His degree is in clinical psychology from Boston University.

Richard Suchinsky, MD, is Associate Chief for Addictive Disorders in the Mental Health Strategic Health Group, Veterans Health Administration, Department of Veterans Affairs (VA). In this position he is responsible for the development and management of substance abuse treatment services provided to veterans in nearly 160 VA medical facilities. In this capacity, he also serves as VA representative on National Advisory Councils of the National Institute of Mental Health, National Institute of Drug Abuse, and National Institute on Alcohol Abuse and Alcoholism. In addition, he served as VA liaison to the White House Office of National Drug Control Policy, the Food and Drug Administration-sponsored interagency council on methadone treatment, and the Department of the Interior Interagency Group on American Indian and Alaska Native Alcohol and Substance Abuse Prevention. Prior to his current appointment, he served as Chief of Psychiatry at the Lakeside VA Medical Center in Chicago. His academic positions include Assistant Professor of Psychiatry at Stanford University School of Medicine, the State University of New York, and Northwestern University Medical School. He has been Associate Professor of Clinical Psychiatry at Cornell University and Georgetown University School of Medicine. For over 20 years, he had a private practice of psychiatry. He also serves as a consultant and has prepared various articles for publication.

About the Contributors

Paul P. Block, PhD, is Instructor of Psychology in the Department of Psychiatry at Harvard Medical School. He also serves as Assistant Chief of the Psychology Service at the Veterans Affairs Medical Center in Brockton and West Roxbury, Massachusetts. Formerly, he was a faculty member at the Graduate School of Professional Psychology at the University of Denver. He founded Lakeside Psychological Services, a brief-therapy community clinic, and the Worcester Veterans Affairs Outpatient Clinic Alcohol Treatment Program. He has served as a member of the Medical and Scientific Advisory Group for a managed mental health company and on the board of a community-based organization providing support groups and other community services related to mental health and psychosocial functioning. He earned his doctorate in clinical psychology at New York University.

John Gillick, PhD, is Chief of the Psychology Service for the Department of Veterans Affairs Western New York Healthcare System. He is an Adjunct Faculty Member for Psychology in the Department of Psychiatry, School of Medicine, at the State University of New York (SUNY) Buffalo and an Adjunct Faculty Member in the Department of Psychology, SUNY Buffalo. He formerly served as the Chief of Substance Abuse Programs and Director of Training at the Buffalo Department of Veterans Affairs Medical Center. With Stephen Schlesinger, PhD, he is the coauthor of *Stop Drinking and Start Living.* He earned his doctorate in clinical psychology at SUNY Buffalo.

Stephen F. Gibson, PhD, is Social Science Analyst at the Department of Veterans Affairs, Brockton/West Roxbury. His past experience includes heading an outpatient alcoholism treatment program at Brockton. More recently, he has had oversight for continuous quality improvement activities, utilization and review, and computer applications for mental health services, including psychiatry, psychology, and social work. He completed his education as a clinical psychologist at the University of Washington and wrote his doctoral dissertation at Brandeis University.

Robert G. Hallett, MSW, is Chief of the Domiciliary Service at the Brockton/West Roxbury Veterans Affairs Medical Center and is responsible for administration and policy development for its homeless rehabilitation program. He is a member of the Medical Center's Clinical Executive Board and Mental Health and Behavioral Council. Previously, he was Program Coordinator for Substance Abuse Services at the Bedford Veterans Affairs Medical Center. Before joining the Department of Veterans Affairs, he held administrative and direct care positions in public and private addictions and mental health treatment facilities. He is a former Clinical Assistant Professor at Smith College and the Boston University School of Social Work and currently serves as the Chairman of the Drug and Alcohol Abuse Committee of the Massachusetts Chapter of the National Association of Social Work. He earned his MSW at the Boston University School of Social Work and is a licensed independent clinical social worker in Massachusetts.

Sigmund Hough, PhD, is Instructor in Psychology in the Department of Psychiatry at the Harvard Medical School and an Associate Graduate Faculty Member at Framingham State College. He serves as the Clinical Neuropsychologist within the Medical Liaison Consultation and Spinal Cord Injury Services at the Brockton/West Roxbury Veterans Affairs Medical Center. He also has a medical staff appointment in the Department of Psychiatry at Melrose-Wakefield Hospital. He has served as Clinical Director and Director of Psychological Services at private rehabilitation facilities, as a case reviewer for a nationwide managed mental health care company, and as a clinical service provider for agencies within both the public and private sectors. His doctorate is in clinical psychology from Boston University.

Norlee K. Manley, RN, MSN, has been a research consultant to the University of Akron Department of Nursing. Previously she served as Deputy Director of the Veterans' Addiction Recovery Center at the Department of Medical Affairs Medical Center in Cleveland and Brecksville, Ohio. She earned her master's degree at the University of Akron.

David B. Mather, PhD, is Clinical Instructor of Psychology in the Department of Psychiatry at the Harvard Medical School and Adjunct Clinical Faculty Member at Antioch New England Graduate School. He serves as Clinical Director of the Domiciliary Service at the Veterans Affairs Medical Center in Brockton and West Roxbury, where he provides clinical oversight for a residential rehabilitation program focused on addictions, psychiatric disabilities, and vocational needs for homeless veterans. Previously, he was Director of Dual Diagnosis and Chemical Dependency Treatment at a private psychiatric hospital in Massachusetts. He has held senior clinical and administrative positions in addictions and psychological treatment programs at the U.S. Navy Hospitals in Portsmouth, Virginia, Newport, Rhode Island, and Roosevelt Roads, Puerto Rico. He earned his doctorate in clinical psychology at the University of Connecticut and is certified in addictions treatment by the American Psychological Association College of Professional Psychology, as well as the American Academy of Health Care Providers in the Addictive Disorders.

Robert J. Rotunda, PhD, is Assistant Professor of Psychology at the University of West Florida. Previously, he was Clinical Coordinator for the Counseling for Alcoholics' Marriages Program at the Veterans Affairs Medical Center in Brockton and West Roxbury, Massachusetts. He has conducted a body of research on marital and family functioning in alcoholic couples, marital and family therapy of addictive disorders, and post-traumatic stress disorder. He earned his doctorate in clinical-community psychology at the University of South Carolina and completed postdoctoral training in behavioral marital therapy at the Harvard Families and Addiction Program.

Margot G. Savage, PhD, completed her undergraduate work at Smith College in 1981 and earned her doctorate in clinical psychology from Temple University in 1988. She then worked at the Palo Alto Veterans Affairs Medical Center, first as Staff Psychologist and then as Assistant Chief of the Drug and Alcohol Rehabilitation Unit. In 1994, she left the VA for part-time private practice, specializing in the treatment of adults with substance abuse and dependence.